P9-CBP-788

PAPA

Hemingway in Key West

PAPA
Hemingway in Key West

James McLendon

K&
YP
THE KETCH & YAWL PRESS

We gratefully acknowledge permission to reprint certain excerpts from the writings of Ernest Hemingway, specifically Charles Scribner's Sons: *To Have and Have Not,* copyright © 1937 Ernest Hemingway; renewal copyright © 1965 Mary Hemingway; *Islands in the Stream,* copyright © Charles Scribner's Sons: *For Whom the Bell Tolls,* copyright © 1940 by Ernest Hemingway; renewal copyright © 1968 Mary Hemingway. From an article in *Holiday,* July 1949, © 1949 The Curtis Publishing Company.

Illustration credits: Betty Bruce (collection), pages 4 top, 13 top and bottom; East Martello Museum, page 12 bottom; courtesy and permission of The Ernest Hemingway Foundation, page 8 bottom, page 11; Everett G. Perpall, page 1 top; Florida State Archives, page 1 bottom; Historical Association of Southern Florida, page 14; Library of Congress, page 12 top; Jerry Miller, page 10 bottom; *Key West Citizen,* page 16 top; Monroe County Public Library, page 3; Midtown Galleries, Inc., pages 2 bottom, 9 bottom; Wright Langley (collection), pages 2 top, 3 top, 5 top and bottom, 6 top and bottom, 7 top and bottom, 8 top, 10 top, 15; © 1989 Wright Langley, pages 9 top, 16 bottom. For information on certain photos, contact Wright Langley Archives, 821 Georgia Street, Key West FL 33040, (305) 294-3156.

Revised Edition, 2006
Third Printing, 2019

Copyright © 1972 by James McLendon (original text)
Copyright © 1990 by Langley Press, Inc. (revision and photo compilation)
Copyright © 2006 by Ketch & Yawl Press, LLC (text and photo revision)

Library of Congress Catalog Card Number: 88-81528

ISBN-10: 0-9788-949-1-X
ISBN-13: 978-0-9788-949-1-7

Previously ISBN 978-0-9788-949-1-7 (trade paperback).
Previously ISBN 0-911607-07-2 and ISBN 0-911607-03-X (trade paperback).
Previously ISBN 0-911607-08-0 (hard cover).

All rights reserved, including rights of reproduction and use in any photo process, or by any electronic, digital or mechanical device, printed or written or oral, or recording for sound or visual reproduction or for use in any knowledge or retrieval system or device, unless permission in writing is obtained from the copyright proprietors.

Cover photograph: Historical Association of Southern Florida
Cover design: Solares Hill Design Group / Joan Langley / Tom Corcoran

Ketch & Yawl, LLC
PO Box 5828, Lakeland FL 33807

For my wife Ann

Contents

Illustrations 9
Acknowledgments 11
Prologue 15
1 All the Low Houses 19
2 It was Great Fun 45
3 The Papa Myth Begins 73
4 *Pilar* 99
5 *To Have and Have Not:* Lessons of Key West 129
6 A Beautiful Blonde in a Black Dress 149
7 The End of the Best Ten Years of His Life 165
Epilogue. 191
Bibliography. 195
Index. 199

Illustrations

(sixteen pages following page 128)

1 (top)	P&O Steamship Dock, Key West Harbor
1 (bottom)	Trevor & Morris Building, Key West
2 (top left)	Hemingway and John Dos Passos
2 (top right)	Waldo Peirce, Charles Thompson, Burge Saunders with tarpon
2 (bottom)	Dock at Fort Jefferson, painting by Waldo Peirce
3 (top)	"Bra" Saunders, "Sully" Sullivan with tarpon
3 (bottom)	The Overseas Hotel, Fleming St., Key West
4 (top)	Samuelson, Juan, Pauline, Carlos Gutierrez, Dr. Henry Fowler, Dr. Charles Cadwalader and Hemingway on *Pilar* in Havana
4 (bottom)	Pauline, John and Katy Dos Passos, Ernest
5 (top)	Pauline Hemingway with sailfish, Charles Thompson, "Sloppy Joe Russell," Cuba
5 (bottom)	Hemingway with marlin, onlookers, Cuba

6 (top)	Charles Thompson with water buffalo, Africa
6 (bottom)	Hemingway with rhinoceros, Africa
7 (top)	Pauline Hemingway with gazelle, Africa
7 (bottom)	Hemingway with lion, Africa
8 (top)	Hemingway with two sailfish
8 (bottom)	*Pilar,* Hemingway's "fishing machine"
9 (top)	James "Iron Baby" Roberts
9 (bottom)	Silver Slipper dance floor at Sloppy Joe's
10 (top)	Ernest, Pauline, and the three boys
10 (bottom)	Hemingway's "poolhouse" workroom
11 (top)	"Sloppy Joe" Russell and Hemingway
11 (bottom)	Painting: Sloppy Joe's Bar on Greene Street
12 (top)	Sloppy Joe's Bar on Duval Street
12 (bottom)	Pool and grounds, Whitehead Street home
13 (top)	Toby Bruce, Patrick and Gregory Hemingway
13 (bottom)	Martha Gellhorn
14 (full)	Hemingway on stairs to workroom
15 (full)	Pauline Hemingway and friends beside Whitehead home poolhouse
16 (top)	*Key West Citizen,* July 3, 1961
16 (bottom)	Ernest Hemingway Museum, Key West

Acknowledgments

No author can hope to thank properly all those who aided him in the completion of his task. Many go unnamed here, and to them my deep and sincere thanks for their help and encouragement over the three and a half years of the project.

I owe a personal as well as professional debt to those persons who generously shared with me their reminiscences of Hemingway in Key West, particularly to Toby Bruce and his wife Betty, and to Charles and Lorine Thompson.

I also owe the following people a large debt for their various services and assistance: Earl Adams, Nilo Albury, R.L. (Bobby) Brown, William Cates, Octavio (Tabby) Cervantes, Charles P. (Junior) Curry, Jr., Jack Daniel, Bernice Dickson, Margaret Foresman, Eugene Hernandez, Donald (Jake) Key, Donald Pinder, Dorothy Raymer, James (Iron Baby) Roberts, Roe Russell, Jr., Stan Smith and Miriam Williams.

In the writing of this book, seven names present themselves almost automatically. They are Dr. Richard Rupp, professor of English, University of Miami at Coral Gables, Florida; Charles

Brock, editor of the *Times-Journal Magazine,* Jacksonville, Florida; Dr. John King, chairman of the department of higher education, Southern Illinois University; Rex Reynolds, University of Chicago; Mrs. Glennie King, rare book librarian, Morris Library, Southern Illinois University; Dr. W. Ann Reynolds, University of Illinois Medical Center at Chicago; and Vernon Sternberg, director, Southern Illinois University Press. Each in their own way—with special acknowledgment to Professor Rupp, who acted as editor and advisor on the book—made its completion successful.

To Adele Head, my secretary, a tireless worker on the project, my complete thanks.

PAPA
Hemingway in Key West

Prologue

That there is a Hemingway Myth, a legend, a code of *machismo* is as sure a thing in American literature as that there is a "Yoknapatawpha County," Mississippi.

But on the one hand Faulkner's fictional county has clearly spelled-out dimensions, a citizenry, cities, towns, and hamlets, and—even though fictionalized—a pinpointed geographical location. The Hemingway Myth, however, while it might have been spelled out and recorded much as Faulkner did with his own hand-drawn map of his country, has been chronicled in a diverse set of biographies, photographs, magazine articles, Hemingway's own journals and nonfiction pieces, stories told and retold by his associates, and, in some instances, pure nonfactual legend, all pieces that never had the clarity, the obviousness, the intent even of the Yoknapatawpha saga.

To further cloud the issue, emphasis thus far on the Hemingway story has been on the years when the myth was in full flower, when Papa reigned with supreme machismo. In the art of literary map-making this is roughly the equivalent of putting road signs along highways that do not exist.

In *Papa* I have attempted a sort of literary highway project—weaving the roads in between the signs that already exist,
concentrating on the years 1928 to 1940, a heretofore obscure
part of Hemingway's life. With the considerable amount of
biographical work already done on Hemingway it may seem
irreverent to propose that the single most important chunk of
the author's life has been passed over and almost obscured to
date. But I do propose this. It is my belief that these years,
1928 to 1940, the dozen years Ernest Hemingway spent as a
permanent or sometime resident in the small seaport town of
Key West, Florida, were the most important years of his life;
they were a time when the Machismo Myth was born—a myth
that allowed Hemingway to move in an aura of self-created
magnificence around the globe.

Whether in Africa, in Cuba, in Spain, or in remote parts of
the American West, Hemingway carried his machismo with
him like a good luck charm. Further, I believe that when
Hemingway arrived in Key West in 1928, a slightly published
28-year-old author, he came searching for his myth, if not consciously then subconsciously. In Key West, a cosmopolitan
backwater that has provided homes for some of America's
finest writers (James Herlihy, Thomas McGuane, Tennessee
Williams, Annie Dillard, Ann Beattie, John Dewey, and others)
with its almost mystical island presence, he found what he was
to become.

It is no accident that that same young Hemingway became
the half-grimacing, half-smiling Hemingway, dressed at various times in plaid shirts, leather vests, white tennis visors,
moccasins, Hong Kong tweed coats, and wool ties; sometimes
sporting an English Army officer's moustache blunted off
smartly at the corners of his mouth, sometimes raising a full
beard that at last turned white and hoary and patriarchal and
became one of the essential Hemingway symbols, along with
his "Gott Mit Uns" World War II belt, white Cuban *guayabera*

shirts, hand-starched, pleated, and worn over his trousers (that were forever cinched up over his considerable midsection by the German belt); and such other equipment as handmade French and Spanish shotguns, an English-made elephant gun, big bore field guns; a 38-foot yacht rigged as impressively as any other craft of its day for fishing marlin; houses in Idaho, Cuba, and Key West; apartments and hotel rooms throughout Europe at his command; and in later years an open invitation from the madam of Havana's number one brothel to personally put his own stamp of approval on its practitioners. And from the late 1920s on, the companionship of a small army of bookies, thugs, bartenders, restauranteurs, soldiers of war and fortune, movie stars, writers, athletes, sportsmen, well-wishers, hangers-on, spongers, and even some genuine friends.

In general, critics, biographers, and casual readers alike have failed to recognize this. In the preface to her *Portrait of Hemingway,* Lillian Ross said it best. "They didn't like Hemingway to be Hemingway. They wanted him to be somebody else—probably themselves." And it was Lillian Ross, among all the Hemingway biographers, both scholarly and popular, who first recognized that Hemingway was indeed his own best story. In every sense he was all he knew.

The proof? After he finally left Key West and his second wife Pauline Pfeiffer in 1940 for Cuba and his third wife Martha Gellhorn, he became involved in journalistic coverage of the World War II battlefronts in Europe. Suddenly a heavily bearded patriarch replaced the jaunty moustached Ernest of only a few years before. With the publication of *For Whom the Bell Tolls,* "Old Man Hemingway," as he called himself (although he was barely 41), fused with that image. He went into a readjustment period and did not publish again for ten years. When he came back in 1950, Hemingway's ego became so closely entwined with Colonel Cantwell (*Across the River and into the Trees*) and Santiago (*The Old Man and the Sea*) that they are sometimes almost indiscernible. After 1940 ego and hero blended in ill-disguised wish-fulfillment. And the germination of that mythic self is unalterably linked to Hemingway's Key West period.

Since I never met Ernest Hemingway, I have been obliged to draw from remembrances of those who knew him, those who wrote about him, and what he wrote about himself.

But I have lived in Key West, his town, and I have made a record of his years there. I did this principally by interviewing his friends and acquaintances still living in Key West, members of what Hemingway called his Key West Mob. Through them the reader will be able to see Hemingway as he formed his myth; he will see the young man on the streets of Key West, living out his boisterous lifestyle, sorting out parts of it for his writing; he will see Hemingway as he grew to national fame; he will see the man become the institution known as "Papa."

Lower Matecumbe Key, Florida
Summer 1972   JAMES MCLENDON

1

All the Low Houses

Key West rose from the Gulf Stream into the raw white sunlight of early subtropical spring. The island appeared first as a blur on the horizon but took shape and definition as the Peninsular & Occidental steamship proceeded northward on approach to the harbor's Southwest Channel. The remote island's tallest building—the seven-story Key West Colonial Hotel—was first to appear to passengers on the forward observation deck of the P. & O. ship, still ten miles out on its 90-mile run from Havana.

The steamship ran out of the Gulf Stream's dark blue-green waters and entered the Southwest Channel, a narrow trough through crystal green and grassy shallows. Sand Key Light, taken to port, quickly fell behind.

Passengers crowded the rails. The plush, sprawling Casa Marina Hotel on the island's south side appeared to the east of the taller La Concha Hotel. Tin roofs of low houses flashed patches of sunlight to the steamship as it rolled gently up the channel. Next in view came the tall, slender radio towers near the main harbor. Gray smoke billowed from a garbage dump recently installed within the ill-maintained brick walls of long-defunct Fort Taylor.

Ernest and Pauline Hemingway stood on the forward deck with the other passengers. The stiff collar of Ernest's shirt was soaked through with perspiration; he tugged resentfully at his tie's large knot. His sandy brown hair was longer than usual and slightly curled over his broad forehead. He wore a full, evenly squared-off moustache. A large purple scar over his right eye, the result of a freak accident—being struck by a falling glass skylight and having to take nine stitches before he and Pauline left Paris only weeks earlier—gave Ernest the appearance of a light-heavyweight prizefighter or of a northern gangster returning from a holiday in Havana.

Dressed in a fresh white lace dress and a matching straw hat that concealed her short, boyish, black hairdo, Pauline seemed small and birdlike beside Ernest, somehow out of place. With the first signs of her five-month pregnancy in evidence, she even looked a little forlorn.

Hemingway watched intently as buildings along the waterfront came into focus. His fellow expatriate writer, John Dos Passos, had described Key West and the 120-mile chain of Florida Keys as "something seen in a dream." At this journey's end, the sea-level, end-of-the-line town presented little more than a backwater appearance.

Ernest continued to gaze at the flat, dilapidated seaport, its apparent lack of character. Off to starboard, behind the tall masts of a large wooden schooner, rose the white spire of St. Paul's Episcopal Church. The Mallory Steamship Company docks appeared to starboard then fell from view. The steamship slowed to enter the dredged central harbor. As the liner reached the island's northwest side, various commercial fish docks and the three massive piers of Trumbo Island presented themselves.

Two large Florida East Coast Railway car ferries, the *Henry*

M. Flagler, a 360-foot behemoth with a 57-foot beam (named for the railroad's founder) and the *Joseph R. Parrott* (for the chief engineer of the FEC's Florida City-to-Key West Overseas Railroad), waited stern first at the two far piers. Each car ferry was fitted with four standard-gauge railroad tracks to accommodate thirty to thirty-five fully loaded (and tightly-secured) freight cars bound for or inbound from Havana.

The P. & O. steamship now turned to full north inside the Key West Bight and angled into position for a berth at the first of the Trumbo piers. Ernest surveyed the bleak-looking FEC train yard that surrounded the steamship, like all train yards bustling and dirty. The noise of steam engines pushing their cargo aboard the car ferries increased. The liner stopped and its sailors secured its dock lines to huge bollards. Ernest and Pauline retreated to their cabin and waited for their luggage to be taken ashore to the customs shed. They would clear customs shortly before noon. Then, leaving Pauline with their considerable luggage, Ernest scouted the immediate area for the Model A Ford that Gustavus Pfeiffer, Pauline's "Uncle Gus," had bought for them.

After Ernest searched in vain for some time he was obliged to call the Ford dealership, the Trevor and Morris Company, located on Simonton Street, 200 feet from its intersection with Caroline Street. He was told that difficulties in ferrying the car from Miami had held up its delivery. The dealership owners not only apologized away the car's absence, but insisted that the Hemingways take up residence in the Trevor and Morris Apartments. Soaked with perspiration and irritated, Ernest did not argue the point; he summoned a taxi to carry their luggage six blocks from the P. & O. docks, down Caroline to the apartment building, a fortresslike, concrete, three-story structure that also housed the dealership.

At first glance, it was not the sort of accommodation the Hemingways had been used to, but Ernest grudgingly signed the register and went off to a drab set of rooms in the rear wing of the second floor; directly above the garage.

They had arrived in Key West at the end of the first week of April, 1928. If taking delivery of the Ford had not been necessary, Ernest and Pauline, like so many tourists before them, might have taken a taxi tour of the island and caught the afternoon train for Miami. But Dos Passos had praised the island city as "just what Ole Hem needed" to "dry out his bones" from a long winter in Paris so that he could continue working on the crumpled pencil manuscript of *A Farewell to Arms* that he had brought with him.

The steamship route from Marseilles via Havana was by far the cheapest way home. But all Key West meant to Ernest in early April, 1928, was the closing of his expatriate era. He had been away for almost seven years.

The subtropical heat was good for Ernest. Despite the confinement of their rooms he set to work almost immediately on his half-finished manuscript. They had no sooner unpacked when Ernest received word on April 10, via mail forwarded from Paris, that his parents were in Florida. Dr. Clarence Hemingway, a physician, and his wife, Grace, were in St. Petersburg inspecting some of Dr. Hemingway's land holdings. Unknown to Ernest, the elder Hemingways had boarded a P. & O. passenger steamship at Port Tampa; after a weekend cruise to Havana, they proceeded to Key West in mid-April. Ernest was fishing from a dock on the Key West waterfront when they arrived. His father, having no idea Ernest had returned from Europe, saw his son and, astounded, gave the family bobwhite whistle to him on the pier below.

Ernest, taken by surprise, looked up to search the nearby waters. When his eyes met his father's he whistled back then dropped his rod and reel and raced the steamship until it docked several hundred yards away at Trumbo pier.

Ernest had a good reunion with his parents on the P. & O. docks, but it was apparent that his father was in ill health. The doctor's full beard had turned gray and his hair was white and lifeless. His diabetic diet and heart condition had taken a severe toll on him since their last meeting, some years before. Ernest's mother, on the other hand, was characteristically robust and dressed immaculately in hat, gloves, and a full-length white dress. Despite their longstanding differences, she and Ernest greeted each other amiably.

Like Ernest and Pauline, Dr. and Mrs. Hemingway had come into Key West from Havana on a morning steamship, but their plans did not include an overnight stop in Key West. Instead they planned to leave on the afternoon FEC train for Miami and make connections there for a pullman berth back to Chicago and Oak Park. Considering the writing task on *A Farewell to Arms* that lay before him, and his open dislike of his mother's company, Ernest did not labor the point by insisting that his parents prolong their stay. Instead, he simply ushered them around to his quarters at the Trevor and Morris Apartments for their first meeting with their new daughter-in-law.

Pauline and Grace got on surprisingly well, even if each was a little reserved. In light of her pregnancy, Dr. Hemingway found Pauline's short, boyish haircut "amusing," but he expressed a fondness for her from the beginning. He wished her a happy life with his son and, being a deeply religious man, he added that he would pray for her happiness and that she have a healthy baby.

The formalities of that first meeting over, Ernest led them all to a nearby restaurant, probably Delmonico's at 218 Duval Street. Delmonico's served a six-course dinner for fifty cents and also offered arroz con pollo, green turtle steak, fish a la minuta, and Spanish garbanzos; representative Cuban and Key West fare.

After the late lunch Ernest returned Pauline to their rooms at the Trevor and Morris Apartments and gave his parents a tour of the island. Although Key West was—and always has been—primarily a nighttime city, there was a good deal to show his parents that afternoon. Both Dr. and Mrs. Hemingway were especially interested in the architecture of the city. Years later Dos Passos remembered that it looked "faintly New England," but more to the point, it was Conch.

Conch architecture was story-and-a-half wood-frame houses with elaborate latticework done by ships' carpenters who from time to time were forced ashore when their ships wrecked in the shallows. There was also a strong Spanish influence in the local architecture, and with few exceptions all the architecture gave a note of lightness.

For their part, the elder Hemingways appeared interested in the numerous quiet lanes, rows of shade trees, and colorful plants. But Grace was opposed to the snail's pace of life.

Ernest and Pauline saw them off on the 5:40 PM train for Miami. As soon as his parents left, Ernest resumed work on the manuscript. Since the early days in Paris when he wrote in his cramped rooms above a sawmill while his first wife Hadley and their son slept, his custom was to begin writing at dawn and finish by noon or no later than 2:00 PM. But writing now above a Ford garage struck Ernest, as he later confided to Charles Thompson—his closest friend in Key West—as the kind of irony he could "damn well do without."

Charles was little more than a year older than Ernest. He was Ernest's height, broad-shouldered but lean, with a thick brush of unruly brownish-blond hair, and a wide, eager smile that put you at ease at once. He had been educated in New York City public schools and at Mt. Pleasant Military Academy in Ossining-on-the-Hudson, New York, but apart from service in the Army of Occupation in 1919, the majority of his twenty-nine years had been spent in his hometown.

In 1928, the Thompson family was one of the most well-to-do families on the island. The three Thompson brothers (Norberg, Karl, and Charles) owned a ship's chandlery, an ice-house, a cigar box factory, and a hardware and tackle shop. In later years they controlled the green sea turtle industry in the Florida Keys and in Central America and processed their catch in their own Granday Canning Company. Charles and Ernest made an instant friendship after a purely chance meeting, but when Ernest and his group left after that first visit, Charles rather sadly commented to his wife Lorine that "it was fun, but we've seen the last of that gang."

To Charles the Hemingways of Paris were plainly and simply too big for their lazy, Latinized seaport city. But for Ernest, the remote island city was exactly small enough. Although Charles did not realize it that time, he was exactly the kind of man Ernest wanted and needed then for a friend—the kind who would make no demands; the kind Ernest could take from—take the bits and pieces he needed for the characters in his novels; the kind Ernest could learn from.

And what Ernest wanted to learn then, what kept him in Key West and kept him coming back, was fishing. Fishing, and the sea, from 1928 until he died in 1961, became a passion with Ernest; although most of the "sea" works were unpublished during his lifetime, the theme dominated his writing in the last years of his life. When he first crossed the emerald-green waters of the Gulf Stream from Cuba to Key West that April, Ernest was captivated by the idea of battling marlin and sailfish from the fighting chairs of charterboats that daily brought in their prizes to hang on racks before their Garrison Bight anchorages.

The friendship with Charles Thompson, and Ernest's first real link with Key West, began with a chance conversation on a hot April day, little more than a week after he and Pauline arrived in the island city. By the time Uncle Gus's Model A Ford finally arrived, more than a week late, Ernest and Pauline had taken a liking to the lazy little seaport. Soon after that, Ernest began daily fishing excursions up Route 1.

He was on one of those afternoon trips, about twenty-eight miles from Key West, fishing from a narrow dock next to the No Name Key ferry landing when George "Georgie" Brooks— waiting for the next boat to arrive from Lower Matecumbe—

spotted the tall, rugged figure leaning against the pier with a large rod and reel in his hand. Ernest's bright purple scar still showed above his right eye, and the hairless scars from the World War I Austrian .420 shell wound were plainly visible above his right knee. In view of Hemingway's battered, moustached appearance, Georgie, the State of Florida's prosecuting attorney for the Keys, probably struck up a conversation to see if Ernest might be another northern gangster or bootlegger on the run.

Without knowing it, Ernest quickly put Georgie's apprehensions to rest when he told the lawyer he was resting up from a "bloody awful" winter in Paris and, he added, "writing a book." He also told Brooks that he was looking for someone with a boat who would be willing to share fishing expenses. Georgie replied that finding a boat in the Keys was a minor problem. At 2:00 PM, as the doubledecked stern-wheeler made its approach across No Name Key Channel, Brooks shook hands with his tall new friend and told him to go by the Thompson Hardware Store on Caroline Street and introduce himself to Charles Thompson.

"He likes to fish as well as any man I know," Georgie said, as he got into his car. "He'll take you out," Brooks added, as he drove onto the creaky wooden ferry ramp. "Just tell him I sent you by."

Ernest waved goodbye to the man who would become one of his prime drinking companions during the Key West years, gathered up his fishing tackle and the few hog snappers he had caught that afternoon, stowed them in the back of the Ford, and rumbled off for the half-hour ride back to town. He walked into the hardware store, suntanned, in a baggy, fish-stained pullover shirt, a cloth fishing cap, canvas walking shorts, and a pair of dingy tennis shoes, looking almost seedy and a little suspect. But eagerness and kindness showed in his face, and Charles responded to him almost on reflex. Charles was standing behind one of the store's half-glass display cases in khakis.

Ernest went right up and asked for him, and they shook hands to begin one of the closest friendships Hemingway ever made, a friendship that for once did not end in a heated argument.

Georgie Brooks, or "Bee-lips," as Ernest labeled him in *To Have and Have Not,* could not have chosen a better companion for Hemingway than Charles, who later became "Old Karl" in *The Green Hills of Africa.* It was a nickname first given him by a German guide on his first hunting trip to the Nordquist L-Bar-T Ranch in Wyoming with Ernest in 1930. Although Charles's older brother—the sheriff in Key West—was named Karl, Ernest persisted in the nickname throughout their relationship. Almost from the beginning they shared the exact kind of sportsman's bond Ernest adopted and wrote about. Their friendship was so close that Charles's wife, Lorine, thought of them as brothers even before Ernest departed that first spring.

Ernest and Charles talked for a while then made arrangements to go fishing the next evening in Thompson's small outboard motorboat. After work that first day, Charles closed the store across from the shrimp docks and walked the few blocks to his white, wood-frame Conch house at 1029 Fleming Street. Over dinner that evening he told Lorine about "a guy who came by the store today."

"Georgie Brooks sent him by," he said. "Says his name's Hemingway. Said Georgie told him I liked to fish and might take him out. Says he's written a couple of books."

"He's going to give me some of them," Charles continued. "I'm taking him out tomorrow. He seems like a heck of a nice guy."

The two new friends went fishing that next evening and caught several good-sized tarpon. They had a rule that when one hooked a fish, the other would quickly reel in and hold a flashlight on the other's line and then gaff the silver flat-nosed tarpon when it was finally wrestled alongside Charles's eighteen-foot motorboat. To keep from running aground in the channel that lay almost due north of the island

off Key West Bight, they hung a lantern on the post where
the channel emptied into the Gulf, an idea recommended by
Ernest.

Charles had the edge at first, but later he was outdistanced
by his new friend because of Ernest's sheer, hardheaded determination to master whatever he did. Six years later, when they
were hunting game in Africa, the situation repeated itself.
Charles again held the edge at first, but Ernest finally got the
hunt's prize trophies near the end of their month-long safari.

The first afternoon of tarpon fishing cemented the friendship, and for their first family get-together, Charles and Lorine
had the Hemingways over for a conch dinner. Phoebe, Lorine's
cook, a black Bahamian woman, cooked green turtle steak,
black beans, and yellow rice, made a raw conch meat salad,
and served heaps of succulent Cuban bread. Ernest brought
over several bottles of good red Chianti and signed copies of
The Sun Also Rises and *Men Without Women.* The inked
inscription on the inside cover of *The Sun Also Rises* read simply, "To Charles Thompson from his friend Ernest
Hemingway, Key West 1928." The inscription in *Men Without
Women* got to the heart of their early relationship with the
words "To Charles Thompson with all best wishes-and many
tarpon-from his friend Ernest Hemingway, Key West 1928."

The dinner went very well, and Ernest showered so many
compliments on Phoebe and her cooking that he was more or
less adopted by the aging black woman, who proclaimed with
much delight, in her strong Bahamian dialect, "That mon
Hemnway one fine eater." After dinner, Ernest delighted his
new friends with stories of his experiences as an 18-year-old
lieutenant and ambulance driver for the Italians during the
First World War, bullfights in Spain, six-day bicycle races in
France, and skiing in the Austrian Alps. Later, he and Charles
had a few scotches in the Thompsons's spacious living room;
then they excused themselves and walked along the shade
trees that lined Fleming Street. They talked about fishing and

hunting and made plans for the remainder of Ernest's stay in Key West.

Lorine and Pauline, who with her pregnancy and fragile size was having considerable difficulty adjusting to the island's heat, moved to the cool, wide front porch and began a friendship as close as the one their husbands were forming. Lorine was the head of the Social Science Department at Key West High School. She had a wide, friendly face, a fine Greek nose, and blue eyes that always seemed inquisitive.

She had graduated from Agnes Scott College in Decatur, Georgia, in 1919, and had come to Key West in 1921 to live with Corrie Woods Higgs, a college friend. She began teaching at the high school that same year and met her husband-to-be through a friend in 1922. They were married on September 6, 1923, in a simple Methodist ceremony. Beside her, Pauline presented an almost tiny figure.

Pauline had recently been a fashion writer on the Paris edition of *Vogue* and was a recent graduate of the University of Missouri in Columbia. She and Lorine found, however, that they had much in common. Both had been born in the backwoods areas of the rural South—Pauline in Piggott, Arkansas, and Lorine in Richland, Georgia—both had graduated from well-recognized southern schools, and each in her own way had gravitated to larger, more cosmopolitan areas. And in a more mysterious, human context, the same chemistry that was working for their husbands was working for them.

Several days after that first dinner with the Hemingways, Lorine was forced to leave Key West to attend her ailing father in Georgia. Her mother, Lorine Betingfield Carter, had called for her help, but when she arrived in Georgia she found her father's condition much improved. After only a brief visit she returned to Key West by train in time to learn that Ernest and Charles—who had fished together nightly in her absence— were about to embark on a weekend fishing trip to the Marquesas Keys.

In Lorine's absence, Ernest had persuaded Charles to leave the hardware store for the weekend. He and Charles had hired Captain Eddie "Bra" Saunders to take them to the islands some 30 miles west of Key West, halfway to the Dry Tortugas. Ernest and Charles brought along a large supply of beer and canned meat, and Ernest also laid in a good supply of his staple diet, juicy Bermuda onions.

Captain Bra was a white Bahamian who had migrated years before to Key West from Green Turtle Key, Bahamas. The sun-creased Conch who was then 42 years old was at home in all the waters from the Cay Sal Banks off Cuba to the treacherous Rebecca Shoals near Tortugas. With the trip, Ernest was in his glory at last, fishing in the waters of the Gulf Stream for sailfish and marlin. *A Farewell to Arms* was going "great guns;" he was over the 50,000 word mark then.

Ernest and Charles and Captain Bra used the safety of the shallow water around the Marquesas Keys as a natural harbor to dock in the evenings, but during the days, Ernest kept them almost constantly in the Gulf Stream a few miles to the southeast. Under Captain Bra's watchful eye, Ernest took his first large sailfish. Each day the leathery-faced charterboatman also made sure that they had a good supply of snapper and yellowtail on board for dinners that he prepared.

All the while Ernest bombarded him with questions about the fishing and the preparation of the fish they caught. He and Charles dived for conchs off the Marquesas to get Captain Bra the ingredients for raw conch salad, a dish that had already become Ernest's favorite. When the three plowed back into Key West on board Bra's charterboat that Sunday afternoon, Pauline and Lorine were on the docks waiting for them, and Pauline remarked to Lorine that she had never before seen Ernest so content.

For her part, Pauline passed an uneventful weekend at Lorine's house. She was suffering in the subtropical heat, and before the baby came she longed for a reunion with her parents and relatives in the cool foothills of Piggott. In truth, she had early confided in Lorine that she had wanted to leave their "tinderbox" apartment from the first. She kept a busy correspondence with friends and relatives back home, and her praises of Key West to her father, Paul Pfeiffer, were so deceptively glowing that he decided to visit them before they ended their stay. He left for Miami from Piggott little more than three weeks after the Hemingways took up their vacation residence on the island. As it turned out, his arrival was simply part of Pauline's plan to abandon the island that had by this time become simply a fishing dock for Ernest.

Paul Pfeiffer was the president of the Piggott Custom Gin Company, where the farmers of surrounding Clay County were obliged to gin their cotton. He was a slightly built man with a round, friendly face. Apart from his cotton processing works, he was also one of the largest landowners in the northeast corner of Arkansas. He and Ernest had a cautious first meeting on the platform of the FEC train station in Key West during the last week of April, 1928. Paul was a highly conservative Catholic, and he had initially taken a dim view of Ernest's divorcing his first wife in 1927 to marry Pauline. The two years from 1925, when Ernest and Pauline first met, until their marriage in Paris in 1927, in the Catholic Church in Passy, had caused Paul Pfeiffer much grief. Now Ernest's suntanned, moustached, aggressive appearance at the train station did little to raise Paul's already doubtful opinion of his new son-in-law.

Ernest and Pauline hustled Paul off to comfortable rooms at the Key West Colonial Hotel at 430 Duval Street, three blocks from the Trevor and Morris Apartments. Later that afternoon Pauline gave her father a tour of the island while Ernest sulked away to a Duval Street speakeasy to console himself with bootleg scotch.

Ernest and Paul got on fairly well, after a slow start. They fished together off the bridges up the Keys, and on several occasions they went fishing with Charles Thompson in his small outboard boat.

Almost from the moment her father arrived, Pauline insisted that she go to Piggott alone on the train for a reunion with her mother before the baby made travel too burdensome. Ernest rebelled at the idea, because it would mean that he would have to drive to Piggott alone in the Ford or with his new father-in-law. Neither prospect, he flatly informed Charles Thompson, appealed to him in the slightest.

He had his way on the matter, with Pauline staying in Key West until the beginning of their fourth week there. But with Paul already in town, and with the heat becoming almost unbearable after noon each day, Pauline prevailed on him to either let her leave or to abandon the island himself and accompany her. Ernest held fast to his refusal of both requests because he and Charles had begun formulating plans for an extended fishing excursion to the Dry Tortugas, 65 miles west of Key West. Still, Pauline persisted in requesting that he allow her to leave, and he finally gave in.

In the chain of events that began with the Model A Ford arriving late, then his meeting Georgie Brooks and Charles Thompson, Pauline's departure probably was one of the most significant occurrences in rooting Ernest to Key West. Although he and Paul Pfeiffer had their relationship on fairly firm footing by this time, Ernest still professed gloom to Charles Thompson at the prospect of spending several weeks alone with his new father-in-law before he followed Pauline to Piggott. All along Ernest had been regaling Charles with both true and tall tales of good times he had spent in Europe in the company of Archibald MacLeish, F. Scott Fitzgerald, and John Dos Passos, and of the fine group of cronies he had assembled at an early age in the lake woods around Horton Bay, Michigan.

Now with his concession to allow Pauline to go to Piggott, Ernest decided to put together a "Mob" in Key West. Even before Pauline left, Ernest sent out letters to his artist friends, Mike Strater and Waldo Peirce; to Bill Smith, a boyhood friend from Horton Bay; and of course to John Dos Passos to join him in the island city he was now calling "The St. Tropez of the Poor." And when they all quickly wrote that they would be down shortly, Pauline seized the opportunity and caught the next FEC train for Miami over Ernest's continued but less heated objections.

Lorine took Pauline to the train station in downtown Key West and put her on an afternoon coach for Miami. She was wearing what Lorine called "A funny little hat, something like a matador's cap, brown and red striped," and a light colored spring suit, knee-length, the height of fashion in Paris. Her father, to Ernest's chagrin, chose to remain behind for what Ernest warned him was a "rough mob" to arrive.

It took Ernest's rough mob little more than a week to assemble in the island city. At once they were joined by what already amounted to his local mob, a group that included Joe Russell, a Conch who owned a charterboat, a speakeasy, and later a bona fide bar that sported his nickname, "Sloppy Joe's;" Captain Eddie Saunders; Burge Saunders, Captain Eddie's half-brother; J.B. Sullivan, a transplanted Irishman who owned a machine shop; Jakie Key, another charterboat captain; Earl "Jewfish" Adams, a newspaperman; Hamilton Adams, a charterboat fisherman; and of course, Charles Thompson, who had long since achieved "mi amigo" status with Ernest.

They were a good-time crowd, and all were ticketed with strange sounding nicknames. J. B. Sullivan was Sully; Dos Passos was Dos; Henry Strater was Mike; Hamilton Adams was Sack of Ham or Sacker; Waldo Peirce was Don Pico; Bill Smith was Old Bill; Joe "Josie" Russell was Sloppy Joe; Captain Eddie Saunders was Bra; and Hemingway was the Mahatma, or Ernie, but most always the Old Master. While in reality he was then far from being the Old Master he became, Ernest was doing everything he could to lay the groundwork for the greatest literary legend this country ever produced.

The mob was installed six blocks from Ernest in dollar-a-day rooms at the Overseas Hotel, a three-story wood-frame 100-room structure at 917 Fleming Street. With its wide, open front porch and wicker rocking chairs, it resembled a large tin-roofed farmhouse.

Nobody remembered the exact day they all were finally assembled, but it was during the first week of May 1928. All week long the temperature had been in the upper 80s; the air was muggy, the sky overcast. *Ben Hur,* billed as "the most beautiful love story of all time," was playing at the Strand Theatre, and a block up on Duval Street Tim McCoy could be seen in *Wyoming* for 25 cents at the Monroe Theater.

Progress on *A Farewell to Arms* was nearing the halfway mark then, but another five months' work remained before a first draft could be completed. The heat and humidity of the island and the confines and noise of the boxlike apartment building made work almost impossible after 10:00 AM, so the book was usually abandoned well before noon for swimming with the Mob at the downtown Navy Yard docks that lay empty as part of President Coolidge's defense cutbacks.

The Mob itself was a rugged looking crew: Waldo Peirce, huge, muscular, with a thick layer of fat around his middle, looked like Robinson Crusoe with his long wirelike full beard and cone-shaped sponge hat. Bill Smith had the tough, stern look of Yankee stubbornness on his oval face that was accented by a tight upper lip. He was about Ernest's height and considerably lighter, but Ernest declared, he was "a feisty sparring partner." John Dos Passos didn't box; he was the observer, average in looks and size, but the most restless and relentless traveler of the group. Then just over 32, he had been around the world once, and was, he claimed, "on my way around again." Charles Thompson, who was tall and lean, with wide, expectant eyes, declared that the Mob was "as grand a group of men as ever came together."

They swam in the deep tropical aqua pools of the Navy Yard basin, and off La Brisa docks at the foot of Simonton Street. The La Brisa docks had for a long time been a favorite of both the Conchs and tourists alike. Only a few locals with connections had access to the Navy Yard, and Charles Thompson, of course, was one of the insiders. To the delight of the others who were always ready for an opening to rile him, Ernest gave less than graceful diving exhibitions off the high board at the foot of the basin, capitalizing—according to Charles Thompson—on his specialty, the "Hemingswan," a crude combination of a swan dive and belly-buster.

But Ernest's performances, and those of the other members of the Mob, went almost unnoticed in the Navy Yard. Defense spending was already being cut drastically. The Key West military community, for over 100 years a flourishing segment of the local economy, was one of the first to feel the cutbacks. Within four years the Navy Yard would be turned into a ghost town (and would remain so from 1932 to 1939).

For dinners, the Mob occasionally met at the Thompsons's Fleming Street house. Phoebe delighted the group with a raw conch salad laced with onions and a spicy Key Lime and salt brine sauce made locally and called Old Sour, a concoction Ernest continually called "Old Oscar." Another mainstay eating location for the Mob was Mrs. Rhoda Baker's Electric Kitchen on the corner of Margaret and Fleming Streets. No matter how modern the name may have sounded, it was the universal appraisal of the Mob that the only things electric about the place were the bare light bulbs suspended from the ceiling. The meals, however, were hearty workingman's portions, and the Mob usually made a daily appearance there at least for breakfast.

After one of Phoebe's dinners the usual routine was to amble down the five blocks from the Thompsons's house to Valladares Book Store at 517 Fleming Street and go through his stacks of magazines, paperbound books, and hardbacks.

The bookstore, owned by a 30-year-old Cuban named Leonte Valladares, was situated in a small, gray, wooden building that had recently been a fishermen's cafe. Valladares and Ernest had met some weeks before, and Hemingway had persuaded him to stock a good supply of hardback books in his store. For his part, Ernest had donated several copies of *The Sun Also Rises* and *Men Without Women* to Valladares, who got a dollar extra on each of the books because they were personally signed by the author.

Valladares's young son Arthur had been the first of the family to see Ernest, and it was Ernest's costume that first attracted the boy's eye. Soon after Ernest arrived in Key West he found or bought a short piece of hemp rope that he knotted through the loops of his trousers (or cut-off shorts) and used as a belt.

He also brought a pair of Indian moccasins with him from Paris (they had been sent to him by friends from Horton Bay), and with this odd combination of clothing he was a character in the eyes of some Key Westers, especially young Valladares. When Arthur first saw him he ran to his father and loudly declaimed in Spanish, "Oh, Father, come look at the poor man."

Ernest heard him and was tremendously amused. He walked over to the boy and in fluent Spanish explained about both the rope belt and the Indian moccasins. The explanation and the fluent Spanish made a lasting impression on both Valladares.

From the bookstore, the Mob normally made the rounds of the downtown speakeasies, usually ending up in a boxlike elbow bar at the foot of Duval Street that sported the owner's nickname of "Sloppy Joe." Joe "Josie" Russell was a red-faced Conch whose charterboat trade complemented impromptu rum-running of "Hoover Gold" from Havana to Key West, a system that worked doubly well when you eliminated the middle man. Josie and Ernest struck up a lasting friendship when the bar owner cashed a Scribner's royalty check for nearly a thousand dollars after a local bank just up the street refused it. Although he staunchly denied he used entire real-life models for his characters, Ernest later immortalized their friendship by using Josie as the model for Freddy, the owner of Freddy's Bar and the charterboat *Queen Conch* in his Key West novel, *To Have and Have Not.*

Although the military was cutting back, Key West, because it was a stopover point for the bibulous Havana-bound vacationer, still hummed. It had its limitations. Geographically, Key West was a nine-square-mile island 120 miles off the U.S. mainland accessible only by ferryboat, railroad, or steamer. Many of its inhabitants still used outdoor privies. All residents were obliged to drink cistern rain water (the water line from the mainland was not installed until the 1940s), but Key West also had its charm. John Dos Passos in 1966, in his *The Best Times,* remembered that on the island in the 1920s, "There were a couple of drowsy hotels where train passengers on their way to Cuba or the Caribbean occasionally stopped over. Palms and pepper trees. The shady streets of unpainted frame houses had a faintly New England look." Dos Passos also said, "In those days Key West was really an island. It was a cooling station. There was shipping in the harbor. The air smelt of the Gulf Stream. It was like no other place in Florida."

It was indeed as Dos Passos suggested, an isolated island, and it was admittedly far from being another Havana, but it was a bit more of an island than one with simply "a couple of drowsy hotels." Small though it was, and with a year-'round population of no more than 11,600, no fewer than four first class hotels, together with many smaller inns and rental rooms, accommodated the transient population.

The Casa Marina Hotel, with its look of rambling European splendor, was built by railroad baron Henry Flagler to coincide with the completion of his Overseas Railroad in 1912 and was by far the best accommodation for travelers on the island.

The winter season hotel boasted several hundred rooms, sculptured grounds, and a boardwalk that looked directly out across the Gulf Stream toward Havana. With most hotel rooms on the island charging around a dollar a day, the Casa Marina's listing of rooms "from $7" limited its clientele to what Hemingway referred to as the "stock and bonds set."

By contrast, the Key West Colonial Hotel (later the La Concha), the Gibson Hotel at 1015 Fleming Street, and the Overseas Hotel at 917 Fleming Street listed lodging on both the European and American Plans from $1 to $6 per day.

Although Prohibition had been in force for over nine years, most of the hotels had speakeasies—"speaks." There were a number of clubs around town where "The Great Experiment" was a total flop. Raul's Club on East Roosevelt Boulevard (formerly the Club Mirimar) was a big favorite with Ernest and his Mob. Raul Vasquez, the owner, had trained a small school of grouper that he had in a tank behind his club. He fed them from his hands like pet dogs, and inside his large story-and-a-half club that afforded an excellent view of the Atlantic from large French windows that circled the building, couples danced on the "finest dance floor in the city" to a live orchestra. Another Mob favorite was Pena Morales's Garden of Roses at 522 Thomas Street (later made part of Truman Annex). Pena's was a pleasant beer garden, a handsome wood-frame structure decked out with much wooden latticework and surrounded aptly enough by a handsome rose garden.

The Mob also frequented the Tropical Club at Front and Fitzpatrick Streets ("where good fellows get together," the sign read) and also spent a number of hours in the Cubana Cafe at 1111 Duval Street, enjoying "Baby's Place" where you could get "foreign and domestic beer—anything you want."

When the Mob ate out as a group they usually chose Delmonico's or Ramon's Restaurant some blocks up at 621 Duval Street. But after only a few hours of making the rounds of the city, Ernest would usually relinquish his position as the

Mob's leader long before midnight, bowing out of the late night drinking because of the early hours he was keeping with *A Farewell to Arms*. Ernest was, after all, still a long way from being "Papa" Hemingway. Just now he was simply another young and dedicated writer working on a good book.

But with the new members of the Mob present, work on the book alternated with fishing excursions and drinking parties. Ernest established a firm policy, dividing his writing time with fishing. Charles bought a second, smaller boat, and the afternoons were taken up with bottom fishing for tarpon, snapper, permit, and jewfish in the channels out from Key West or off nearby Man and Woman Keys. The Mob lazed around Key West through the hot, humid days of early May, but by the start of the third week, Ernest had finally organized his long-awaited trip to the Dry Tortugas Islands. Charles Thompson could leave the hardware store only for a weekend, so Ernest revamped his plans to include a weekend stopover halfway to the Tortugas at the Marquesas Keys.

Ernest again hired Captain Bra Saunders and his charterboat, and Captain Bra's half-brother, Burge, went along as mate. On Friday afternoon of the third week in May, Ernest, Dos, Archie, Waldo, and Mike Strater on board Captain Bra's boat, with Charles Thompson and Burge bringing up the rear in Charles's 18-foot outboard boat, all finally set out.

They arrived at the Marquesas just before dusk and were able to lay in a good supply of eating fish before dark. Captain Bra and Burge cooked up a fine meal that first night on board Bra's charterboat, and after dinner the Mob drank part of a demijohn of rum and swam in the crystal-clear shallows where the boat was anchored. They were up at dawn for a breakfast of almost syrup-thick, burnt-sugar-tasting Cuban coffee and slices of stale Cuban bread, avocados, and smoked fish; and before the sun had been up for more than an hour, they were out in the two boats after the prize of the Marquesas: giant tarpon.

Bearded Waldo Peirce—"Don Pico"—was a runaway choice for the tarpon record while they were camped at the Marquesas, boating a silver monster that weighed 138-1/2 pounds. The tarpon put up such a battle—it lasted for almost two hours—that when Waldo finally pulled it ashore, he threw Ernest the rod and reel and leaped on the beaten fish in the ankle-deep water and wrestled him into final submission while Bill Smith recorded the whole event with his camera. Near sunset Ernest and Dos Passos shot at sand sharks in the mangrove shallows and potted several luckless white-crowned pigeons and seagulls.

The jaunt in the Marquesas was abandoned early Sunday morning, however, when a low-pressure ridge began moving in from the Gulf of Mexico. Charles departed for Key West alone in his small wooden boat over Ernest's heated protests. Charles made for the safety of the lakes region between the Marquesas and the outlying Man and Woman Keys off Key West, but he had been gone less than an hour when Ernest demanded that Captain Bra, who was then putting his boat in order for the final run to Tortugas, make a circle through the lakes to be certain that Charles was safe.

Captain Bra agreed and gave chase after Charles, but the search was abandoned when they met a group of charterboatmen who had just seen Charles pass through the lakes on his way to Key West. The final run to the Dry Tortugas began then in the treacherous shallows of the lakes, and it was almost dark before Captain Bra tied up at the historic Fort Jefferson docks in Tortugas.

Fort Jefferson, originally designed in 1846 as a defense outpost for the southernmost waters of the United States and a coaling station for ships traveling to and from the Caribbean, was under construction until 1876, but further building was abandoned when ships and the times themselves ruled the awesome structure obsolete. The half-mile perimeter of the brick fort, totaling over 50 million bricks, took up most of the land space on the island of Garden Key. The fort had been in Federal hands throughout the American Civil War, and served as a prison until 1873, housing Dr. Samuel Mudd, the ill-fated Maryland physician who set the leg of John Wilkes Booth.

By sharp contrast, nearby Loggerhead Key and its 1858 lighthouse, sand dune beaches, quiet swaying Australian pines, and palm trees seemed almost virgin as it stood raised just above clear waters fed by both the Gulf Stream and the Atlantic Ocean.

The Mob alternated their headquarters on Captain Bra's boat between the fort and Loggerhead Key, and Waldo Peirce, in spite of his success in the Marquesas, immediately set the Mob record for the most tarpon lost in the Tortugas. Before the trip ended, his total stood at seven. Finally he hooked and landed his eighth, but only after a battle that lasted almost an hour.

Ernest hooked and lost what might have been a prize-winning sailfish, and Bill Smith and Dos all caught nice sized tarpon. The entire party daily took in a good quantity of snapper, yellowtail, and the like, plus raw conch and fresh crawfish that were yanked from underwater rock piles by Waldo who emerged, "beard and belly," like a modern-day Poseidon.

The night before their return trip to Key West, as they sat swapping yarns on the Fort Jefferson docks, Captain Bra told the five the story of the Spanish ocean liner, *Val Banera,* that had been blown off its course in the big Keys hurricane of 1919. The liner, with a crew and passenger list of over 500, foundered and ran aground in the shallows south-southwest of Key West near the Rebecca Light. Captain Bra's boat was the first to reach the doomed ship, and he tried without success to break open the portholes and get at the highly valuable cargo inside. The shipwreck, and Bra's story of seeing a dead woman floating inside a stateroom with a fortune in diamonds on her hand, later became the basis of Ernest's short story, "After the Storm."

The Conch fisherman did not know it that evening, and of course Ernest had no specific design then, but Ernest did more than just listen to a fisherman's tale; he was cataloging all he saw and heard for his writing. While they fished, he especially noticed the man's hands, gnarled and suncreased as they were and accustomed to countless chores at sea, beginning to "freeze up" on him. Ernest made a special effort to point this fact out to Charles Thompson, who passed it off as "rheumatism." But whatever caused the condition was not what interested Ernest. He saw a sadness and a sense of finality in a fisherman who was dependent on two good hands to ply his trade.

More than 20 years later the memories of that first trip to Tortugas came back to Ernest, and Captain Bra's hands became the ailing hands of another fisherman, Santiago, in Ernest's classic *The Old Man and the Sea.* The transformation from one fisherman to another was in keeping with Ernest's practice of taking bits and pieces from the people he knew in order to form one character. Thus in 1928, on a remote island in the Gulf Stream—while the others were simply on a fishing trip—Ernest, consciously or unconsciously, was taking those "bits and pieces" he would use for the rest of his life in his writing.

The following morning the Mob left the Fort Jefferson docks and plowed their way back the nearly ten-hour ride in Captain Bra's charterboat, with Ernest already planning another trip. But that trip would have to wait until the next season because, unlike Ernest, his Mob could remain in Key West for only three weeks. By the last week in May all of the out-of-town Mob members had been given send-offs by Ernest and Charles Thompson on FEC trains. But at a going-away dinner at Charles Thompson's house for Dos Passos, they all agreed to return the following year. Ernest capped the agreement by instructing Lorine Thompson (who believed it was only a courteous request that would not be honored) to find him and Pauline a house for the coming winter season.

With his cronies gone Ernest was outwardly glum. Soon after they had all departed, his dissatisfaction with the heat and what he described to Charles Thompson as amounting to a general case of the "miseries" at being once more stranded with his father-in-law, he too decided it was time to leave.

So with his worked-over manuscript tucked away in the bottom of a suitcase, Ernest and Paul Pfeiffer left Key West for the first time, after a stay of just over seven weeks. Leaving Key West by automobile was no easy task, though. In 1928, after six years' work, there still remained two water gaps in US 1, the Overseas Highway.

In all there were over 26 miles of sea from No Name Key to Lower Matecumbe that were inaccessible to automobile. The biggest gap was the 13 miles between Knights Key (near present-day Marathon) and Big Pine Key, an area that included the present Seven Mile Bridge (then the seven-mile railbed of the FEC) and the present Bahia Honda Bridge (likewise the railbed of the FEC). This area was served by ferry system from No Name Key to Lower Matecumbe, a distance of 41 miles. Leaving that first time, Ernest drove the Ford up US 1 to the No Name Key ferry dock, and with Paul beside him, caught the 9:00 AM ferry for $2 to Lower Matecumbe. When they docked at a point just south of Islamorada at 2:00 PM, they proceeded north on the connecting arm of US 1 over a series of narrow, often rickety concrete and wood bridges, finally crossing the long wooden bridge at Ocean Reef then onto the mainland at Florida City, arriving just before sunset.

Hemingway's thoughts from his 1,400-mile trip to Piggott are lost forever, but he would be gone from Key West just over six months. He must have been putting his recent experiences in some kind of order: the island, the fishing, his Mob of new and old friends, the look, the feel of the entire experience—all this he must have sorted out in his mind. He must have sensed that there was something unique in Key West, something about it that he had been seeking for the past ten years. Undoubtedly he meant to return to Key West. For the next six months a steady stream of letters flowed back to Charles and Lorine Thompson on the small dot at the tip end of America that he was already calling home.

2

It Was Great Fun

Ernest and Paul arrived in Piggott about a week after leaving Key West during the early days of June, tired and dust-covered from the last few hundred miles they had driven on that final day. Ernest had a somewhat cautious first meeting with Mary Pfeiffer, Pauline's mother. As a staunch Catholic, Mary had been vigorously opposed to her daughter's union with Ernest; now Ernest's grizzled appearance did little to soften her resentment.

After weeks of fishing with Ernest, Paul's admiration for his new son-in-law had smoothed over the rough edges of that first meeting. It paved the way for the immediate friendship Ernest made with Gustavus A. Pfeiffer, "Uncle Gus," a friendship that was of major importance as he was the patriarch of the family and one of the richest men in Arkansas. The foundation of Gustavus Pfeiffer's wealth was the controlling interest in Hudnut Perfumes. Like the other Pfeiffers, he was also a considerable landowner in the northeast tip of Arkansas near the Missouri state line. Uncle Gus took an instant liking to the burly and moustached Hemingway, and he greatly admired the fact that Ernest had assigned a good portion of the royalties of *Men Without Women,* then selling over the 20,000 mark, to his former wife Hadley and their son John.

But after the discovery of Key West, the backwoods town of Piggott seemed more than simply 1,400 miles from the pleasure of fishing the Gulf Stream and roaming from one speakeasy to another; it was a rural world of "good ole boys" sitting on dusty cane-back chairs in front of feed stores and filling stations. After a respectful and short visit with his in-laws, Ernest and Pauline departed for Kansas City, Missouri, to stay with friends while Pauline waited for her baby. They stayed in a pleasant little house in a wooded section of the city with Malcolm and Ruth Lowry, old friends of Pauline. Ernest continued work on *A Farewell to Arms* and worked out in a downtown gym.

Pauline had her baby by caesarean section on June 28, 1928, at the Research Hospital in downtown Kansas City. The child, named Patrick, weighed nine and a half pounds. It was mid-July before mother and child were able to travel by train back to Piggott to present the child to the eager grandparents. When the new Hemingway family left Kansas City, *A Farewell to Arms* was almost complete. Ernest was becoming impatient to finish the novel despite, he complained, the confusion of "all this childbirth and heat" in a sweltering summer that seemed to follow him wherever he went.

When they returned to Piggott, Pauline and Ernest took up sleeping quarters in an abandoned barn behind the Pfeiffer house. The unpainted wood structure had been hurriedly converted into a studio chiefly to give Ernest privacy while he wrote. But Ernest's distaste for Piggott remained unchanged; about the only real pleasure he got out of that return trip to Piggott was trap shooting with the local furniture maker who remodeled the barn. The furniture maker's name was T. Otto "Toby" Bruce.

Toby was about half Ernest's size and only eighteen, eleven

years his junior, but he had a pleasant, reassuring smile, and a confident manner that Ernest immediately took to. Like the chance meeting with Charles Thompson four months before, the friendship with "Tobes," as Ernest soon dubbed him, would last the rest of Ernest's life. Toby would become the "Old Master's" man-Friday, driver, money holder, and secretary from 1936 in a sort of off-and-on fashion until "Papa's" death in 1961. For the moment, in the waning summer of 1928, they were two new friends "whooping it up in the woods" like boys on a lark.

The friendship blossomed when Ernest asked Toby to throw skeet targets for him. The new friend put the "big stranger from Paris" (for that was how he and Pauline were being introduced around Piggott—largely at Pauline's insistence, because Ernest was already corresponding with Charles Thompson, telling him of his intention to return to Key West, not the Paris Pauline longed for) to the test. He never threw balls in the same pattern twice. Sometimes the target balls flew out front, sometimes over Ernest's head, and sometimes almost straight up in the air. But Ernest performed like the excellent wing shot he was, and seldom if ever missed the mark.

The two parted fast friends after Ernest's visit yet would not meet again until the fall of 1935. Shortly after Ernest and Pauline left town, Toby went West to work on the railroad in California.

While Ernest was away from Key West that first time, he also had a taste of mountain hunting in Wyoming, and fishing and "dude ranching" with his old World War I ambulance corps compatriot Bill Horne. *A Farewell to Arms* was finished in first draft in a tattered pencil manuscript before he returned to Key West by car with Pauline and baby Patrick.

Ernest was at once anxious to have the manuscript typed and do the second revisions with the hope that he could have the novel ready for Scribner's 1929 spring list. But one final chore remained before he could begin work on the book. John

"Bumby" Hemingway was crossing the Atlantic to spend the winter season in Florida with his father. The boy was barely five years old, but he was, Ernest told Charles Thompson, "as healthy as a bull, and a swell kid." Ernest planned to go to New York City to meet the boy's ship and escort him to Key West for the season, then take Pauline and their new baby to France in the spring to return Bumby to his mother.

In Key West Lorine Thompson had secured Ernest and Pauline a white wood-frame house at 1100 South Street for $100 per month, and had acquired the services of a black woman named Olive to act as Patrick's nurse when they arrived in the city. The typing of the manuscript was to be done by Ernest's twenty-four year old sister Madelaine, called "Sunny," who, it was agreed, would also help tend to Bumby. Ernest left Key West in late November to meet Bumby's ship. Death would delay his return until the Christmas holidays.

On December 6, 1928, Ernest's father, Dr. Clarence Hemingway, committed suicide. The elder Hemingway had been sick for years with diabetes and a heart condition, and on that bleak Chicago winter day, he put a pistol to his head and took his life. Ernest was on a train with young Bumby bound for Key West when the news reached him. He put Bumby, who had only just crossed the Atlantic alone, in the care of an aged black porter, got off the train in mid-journey, and rerouted himself to Chicago for the funeral.

The circumstances caught Ernest short of money, and while Scribner's then was willing to serialize *A Farewell to Arms* for $16,000 sight unseen, he was obliged to wire Mike Strater and Scott Fitzgerald for loans to complete the trip. Dispirited and shaken, faced with the arduous task of rewriting his novel, Ernest returned to Key West just before Christmas.

He immediately blocked from his mind the tragic events surrounding his father's death and the Christmas confusion and worked on the revision of *A Farewell to Arms* from 6:00 AM until noon for five straight weeks in a rear bedroom of the

South Street house. Pauline and Ernest's sister Sunny under-
took the arduous task of typing the manuscript. It was finished
to Ernest's satisfaction on January 22, 1929. Maxwell Perkins,
his Scribner's editor, came to Key West a week later to collect
the typescript and was overjoyed at what he read. The serial
rights to the book were picked up by *Scribner's Magazine* and,
for the first time in his two-year marriage to Pauline, Ernest
contributed meaningfully to their support.

For the two months during which his novel was being set
into galley proofs in New York, Ernest's single concern was
fishing. As they had promised, Mike Strater, Waldo Peirce,
John Dos Passos, and now Max Perkins, came down for the
festivities.

Perkins, a sober New Englander who had connected Scott
Fitzgerald with Scribner's, was about to begin his tortuous
association with the flamboyant, voluminous Thomas Wolfe.
He stood in awe and fascination of the brawny Hemingway
and his boisterous companions; Gulf Stream fishing captivated him as it might a little boy.

Charles Thompson had felt sorry for Max, "cooped up
almost year-round in his New York office. He came down pale
and tired, but when he left, he was tanned and fit," Thompson
proclaimed happily to the Mob. Like the rest of the Mob,
Perkins was ticketed with a nickname: "Deadpan."

Mike Strater, Dos, Waldo, and Max at once decided on a
week-long trip to the Dry Tortugas in Captain Bra's charterboat, but they were delayed a few days while Captain Bra
located his half-brother, Burge. While they waited for Burge,
Dos nosed around the city with Mike and was fascinated by
the Cuban cigar factory workers who hired "readers" to sit at
the ends of their work tables and read novels and daily newspapers to them while they rolled cigars.

The Mob finally rounded up Burge and set out for the
Tortugas with several bottles of good French champagne in
Captain Bra's iced bait boxes. They made a firm rule from the

start. No champagne drinking until they caught fish. The rule was kept, but the fishing was so good that the champagne was soon gone. They fished for a week in and around Fort Jefferson and Loggerhead Key, sleeping on Captain Bra's boat and on the docks at the Fort.

Max was delighted with the fishing and the food, mostly yellowtail, fried crawfish, and raw conch. And he was fascinated by the crystal-clear channels around the island fort. Ocean streams afforded perfect vision to sixty feet and beyond as the tributaries stretched farther out into the depths.

On the night before their return to Key West, Captain Bra and Burge were cooking up one of their usual feasts when a small motor-sailer, a Cuban fishing dinghy with a weathered canvas top, pulled alongside the Mob's dockage at the fort. Ernest began at once to converse with the Cubans in acceptable, even fluent Spanish. Immediately impressed by the fishing knowledge of their captain, Ernest invited both the captain and his small crew over for some rum.

The Cubans drank the rum and afterward ate the last of the feast; then the entire group settled in a circle on the wooden dock in the shadow of the decaying plank boathouse and began to swap yarns about the Gulf Stream. The Cuban captain told of 20-foot rattlesnakes that swam off the Cuban coast and of crocodiles in the Gulf of Mexico, floating lazily many miles out at sea. Captain Bra matched the Cubans' stories with tales of the early white settlers in the Bahamas, and then Ernest topped off the evening by putting on a flawless shooting exhibition for the entire group. He shot targets from almost every conceivable position-even on his head—and never missed.

The Cubans and Max sat speechless, and then the captain, Gutiérrez, produced a wicker-covered container of Aguardiente which was much like bootleg rum; it was still "green" and much over 100 proof. The Mob could not refuse the hospitality of the captain and forced down several rounds of "jug passing" before the Cubans departed to moor off the fort for the night. But Ernest had not been too affected by the Aguardiente to get the captain's name. "Carlos Gutiérrez, Zapate, 31, Havana, Cuba," he recorded. Like Captain Bra, Carlos became a fishing advisor to Ernest and subsequently served as a mate on several of the charterboats Ernest rented, and at times on board the *Pilar*.

The Mahatma, Dos, Don Pico, Mike, Deadpan, Bra, and Burge all passed a sleepless night while the spirits rolled in their stomachs; they were still feeling the effects of the "farewell drink" when Charles Thompson met them as they docked at Garrison Bight in Key West late the next evening.

Max Perkins remained in Key West for a few days after the fishing trip and then reluctantly and over Ernest's objections took the FEC train to Miami for connections to New York. Ernest, however, continued to squire his Mob of writers and artists around town. For the first time, he began to attract public attention. Predictably enough, he had escaped notoriety on his first visit the year before. But now with so many notables coming and going at the South Street address, and advance publicity by Scribner's on the impending publication of *A Farewell to Arms,* Ernest began to attract a horde of newspaper men as well as curiosity seekers.

Being a former newspaper man, Ernest had an easy rapport with most journalists and held forth for many a sidewalk audience along Duval Street or in one of the Duval Street speakeasies with his special brand of staccato candor. But Lorine Thompson liked to warn newsmen that he could be "short," and even on occasion "very nasty."

Ernest's chief tormentors were reporters from out-of-town papers who used him mainly as an excuse to bask in the Key West winter sunshine while their colleagues remained snowbound with deadlines on northern news desks. The local news agencies in Key West—like the Key Westers—generally allowed him the privacy he desired.

Ernest's closest friend among Key West newsmen in those

days, and a friend who remained close to him until his death in 1961, was Earl Adams. Some few years Ernest's junior, Earl was tall, with a head of thick, curly black hair. During his newspaper career he had worked for the local *Key West Morning Journal,* the *Key West Citizen,* the *Baltimore International News,* and was Keys bureau chief for the *Miami Herald.*

When he and Ernest first met in 1929, Earl was holding down the *Herald* bureau job in Key West from an office in his home at 917 Angela Street. Like Ernest's meeting the year before with Georgie Brooks on the No Name Key Bridge, the acquaintance with Earl also was struck up on a bridge out from Key West.

One day in early March, 1929, Ernest was fishing alone on the Niles Key Bridge, only a short distance from the No Name Key Bridge. Near the end of the afternoon he ran out of bait. Earl was fishing on the other side of the bridge, and noticed the "big, tough looking stranger with a bushy moustache" looking in vain through his gear for some bait. He walked over and gave Ernest a handful of bait mullet. They introduced themselves and struck up a conversation. Earl found Ernest "sincere" and understood from the start that "here was a man, if he was your friend, he was your friend. But if he didn't care for you—watch out." For his part, Ernest took an immediate liking to Earl. They swapped yarns about the newspaper business and writing, and exchanged fishing advice; before they parted company there on the bridge that evening, each—thanks to Earl's bait—had caught several nice tarpon.

Over the years, Ernest shared a good many yarns with Earl, some with the understanding that they would remain out of print and others that were given to him as "scoops." One of the confidential stories was about the one-round fight Ernest had in 1936 with the great American poet, Wallace Stevens. (More on that in Chapter Five.) Some years later when Earl quit the *Herald* to run for the Monroe County Circuit Court Clerk's

Office, Ernest, who had always admired his newspaper style, told him he thought he was a "damn fool to leave the newspaper business." When Earl won the election, Ernest muttered his congratulations, but reiterated that he should have stayed in the newspaper "racket."

His temporary exile finally resolved, Ernest came out of hiding and gathered his now considerable family (Sunny, Pauline, the infant Patrick, and Bumby) for the crossing to Havana and the ocean voyage to return Bumby to his mother. Ernest's going-away party at Charles Thompson's ended with instructions that the Thompsons find him another house—"a much bigger house," he specified.

It would be ten months before Ernest would be back in Key West. When he returned the following February, he would have achieved national fame. When *A Farewell to Arms,* was published by Charles Scribner's Sons on September 27, 1929, it paved the way for him to receive $24,000 in movie rights to the book; it also was done as a Broadway play. *A Farewell to Arms* made the bestseller lists that fall and by November 8, 1929, Max Perkins could write Charles Thompson in Key West that "the book is going admirably well." Thinking of the pleasures he had recently enjoyed with the Mob, he added, "There is not much I would rather do than get in another ten days of such a vacation as I had last year."

Ernest, Pauline, Patrick, and Sunny did not prolong their European visit and left Paris during the second week in January 1930, reaching Key West during the first week in February. They went immediately to a large single-story frame house Lorine Thompson had found for them for $100 a month rent on Pearl Street near a gambling casino (a section of Pearl Street that no longer exists, being now a junior high school campus off José Marti Drive). Sunny soon departed, and Ernest settled down to family life with Pauline and Patrick, who was then a healthy nineteen months old.

By mid-March, most of the Mob had again migrated to the

island. Plans for another long fishing trip to the Dry Tortugas were being finalized, hinging only on Max Perkins's arrival from his editorial desk in New York. Ernest had rented a good-sized cabin cruiser "that needed painting but wouldn't sink," he said, and Burge Saunders had agreed once again to serve as a one-man crew and guide. Mike Strater joined the group once more and found time to paint Ernest's portrait as he sat looking cocky, heavily moustached, and wearing a dark blue shirt. John Herrmann, a writer Ernest met in Paris in 1924, whose novel *What Happens* was so rough for the age that it had been barred from the States, made up the last of the fishing Mob.

The Mob boarded the boat a few days after the fifteenth of March and trolled easily from Key West to the Marquesas Keys, taking a good number of sailfish. Max Perkins astonished himself and the rest of the crew by boating a 58-pound kingfish, one pound over the current record for a king caught on a rod and reel. But the trip that was supposed to last a week stretched into seventeen days. The Mob was virtually marooned on the Fort Jefferson docks because of a fierce tropical storm. They had taken an ample supply of canned goods, beer, coffee, liquor, and Ernest's Bermuda onions, but the seventeen days exhausted the food chest and in the end their diet was reduced to fish.

An anxious group of wives greeted the bearded group when they returned to Key West during the first week of April, but Ernest later bragged that Pauline had not worried over his absence. Max shaved and caught the next train for New York but he was none too happy to leave. As Charles Thompson drove him to the train station, he expounded mightily on what he repeatedly called "a grand adventure," and as he boarded the train he turned to Charles and said, "This town is certainly good for Ernest."

"I hope he thinks so," Charles replied. "I don't know what we'd do around here without him."

After the fishing trip, Ernest's attentions turned to two

long-anticipated projects: a safari into Kenya and Tanganyika, and work on a nonfiction book about bullfighting, the sport he had observed most recently during the past fall in Spain, and with great interest generally since his early days in Paris.

He began work on the bullfight book in Key West, but in early June with the island's heat closing in, he packed Pauline and Patrick and Patrick's French nurse off to Piggott. He then drove the Ford alone to New York to meet Bumby, who had again sailed from France for another summer with his father. But before he left he and Charles toured the island several times with the express mission of looking for what Ernest described as "a place to hang my hat."

"You don't have a hat," Charles needled him.

"Well by God, I'll buy one the day I move in," Ernest replied.

They did not succeed in finding a house that met Hemingway's approval, but Charles did not press the point. Unknown to Ernest, Pauline and Lorine Thompson had also made several rounds of the city before she entrained for Piggott. On one of the trips, Lorine took Pauline to a large vacant lot on the ocean on the eastern side of the island. It was fairly isolated (near the present West Martello Towers) and accessible only by a rough coral road and dotted with fully grown palm trees.

"You and Ernest could build something tailor-made to your own tastes," she suggested.

But Pauline immediately rejected the idea.

"Ernest and I both like old houses," she said. "We want something we can fix up."

With the Depression already having an adverse effect on the island, there were a number of houses that fit Pauline's specifications. She and Lorine toured several barnlike two-story houses in the center of town and even stopped by what Lorine initially described as a "miserable wreck of a house on Whitehead Street." The house was at 907 Whitehead. It was a much-neglected white stone dwelling with only a sparse collection of scraggly palm trees in its large, almost grassless, yard.

The house had been a casualty of the Depression and was in a state of gross ill-repair. Lorine and Pauline managed to get into a back entrance, but their impromptu inspection was immediately cut short because some of the ceiling plaster chipped and fell into Pauline's eye. Ironically, Pauline left the house she and Ernest would buy in 1931, cursing and calling it "a damned haunted house."

In New York, Ernest collected Bumby-now a handsome, chunky six-year-old-and ordered a custom-made 6.5mm Mannlicher rifle for his proposed African safari. Then he drove across country to Piggott with the boy as passenger. By mid-July, "The Pig had gotten him," he said of Piggott, and he, Pauline, and Bumby (Patrick stayed with his grandmother in Arkansas) moved West, searching for a cool place for him to write and a place for some warm-up hunting for the African safari he was "itching for."

They settled in a log cabin on the Nordquist L-Bar-T Dude Ranch on the Clark Fork branch of the Yellowstone River in Wyoming, and Ernest soon eased into his habitual routine of fishing and hunting and writing, in what he described as a "beauty place."

By the last week in October, the bullfight book he would call *Death in the Afternoon* was becoming a creditable pile of manuscript in the bedroom of his log cabin at the ranch, and he felt sufficiently at ease to take a break from the writing. He and Floyd Allington, an L-Bar-T ranch hand, met Dos Passos by prearrangement in Billings, Montana, for ten days of elk hunting in the Crazy Lakes region.

They had a "heap big powwow," he later told Charles Thompson, but on their way back to Nordquist Ranch, a freak automobile mishap postponed his plans for the coming year. Driving his Model A Ford on a mountain road just before sunset, blinded by the lights of an oncoming car, Ernest drove into a ditch. As always, he got the worst end of the accident. When Dos and Floyd, both virtually uninjured, pulled him from the Ford, Ernest had a broken right arm. After an operation on the arm at St. Vincent's Hospital in Billings some days later, Ernest dictated a letter to Charles Thompson. With a shaky left hand he signed it with the sum of his feelings at the time: "poor ole Papa," he wrote, referring to himself as he had privately since the birth of his son John. Why he called himself Papa was unclear to the Thompsons—who knew him only as Ernest or by the nicknames conferred on him by his Key West Mob—but it stuck in their memories.

He was released from the hospital just before the 1930 Christmas holidays, and he and Pauline went by train to Piggott, but they soon departed for Key West, where the Thompsons had already made arrangements for their arrival. When he returned to Key West he was Ernest and not Papa, but soon he would have it clearly spelled out and, with Pauline's help, the change from Ernest to Papa would occur before his thirty-sixth birthday.

Key West had now become the Hemingway's January-to-June home. For their third house, Lorine Thompson secured a large, two-story, wood-frame Conch house on the corner of Whitehead and United Streets, only one block from what was being billed as the "Southernmost Point in the U.S.A." The house was owned by Fannie Curry and was rented to the Hemingways for $130 per month.

Shortly after Ernest arrived, Dos Passos advised him that he could not make it down for the third season, but the Mob functioned as heartily as ever, chiefly around the new group of cronies Ernest had acquired on his trip out West. Lawrence and Olive Nordquist, the owners of the Wyoming L-Bar-T Dude Ranch, having been regaled by "Hemingversions" of the pleasures of Key West, came into town to join him. John Herrmann, "the dirty book specialist," as Ernest dubbed him, and his wife Josie were there, as well as Chub Weaver, the L-Bar-T ranch hand who had driven the crippled Ford to Key West after the Montana accident. Ernest's mother came in for a few days, and his 20-year-old sister Carol—a college student in upstate Florida—also was there. And, of course, the regulars: Charles Thompson and his wife Lorine, Sully Sullivan, Sloppy Joe Russell, Captain Bra, and Burge.

Despite his injured arm, Ernest, with Charles Thompson, made several crossings to Havana with Joe Russell on marlin fishing expeditions aboard Sloppy Joe's charterboat *Anita*. They all stayed at the Ambos Mundos Hotel near the San Francisco docks; each time they took the *Anita* into the Gulf Stream they had good luck, boating many large sailfish.

Ernest, who as always was both participant and observer, had some important and private luck of his own on one of the fishing trips as an outgrowth of an incident that seemed trivial to Charles and Joe Russell. A small yellow and green "love bird" happened to light on the *Anita's* deck while they were miles out at sea in the Gulf Stream from Havana harbor. The tiny bird was so exhausted that Charles had no trouble simply walking over to it, picking it up, and finally anchoring it to the boat with a piece of twine. No one paid much attention to the bird during the rest of the day's fishing, but Charles carried the small creature with him when they returned to their rooms at the Ambos Mundos Hotel that afternoon. Charles still had the small bird held fast with the twine around one of its spindly legs when he and Joe and Ernest went out for drinks that night in the row of bars down from their hotel. But with all the drinking that followed, Charles almost lost his prize when the twine slipped off the bird's legs.

"But quick as a flash," he said later, "some guy in the bar jumped up across from us and grabbed the little fellow like he had on a catcher's mitt."

Later, Charles had a wicker cage made for the bird, but it soon died. "Our cat never gave the poor thing a minute's peace, and finally it died of a nervous fit or something," Lorine said.

The part Ernest remembered about the small bird was simply that it was almost totally exhausted when it landed on the boat far out in the Gulf Stream. In his novel *The Old Man and the Sea,* written more than 20 years later, a small exhausted yellow bird lands on the deck of the old fisherman's dinghy. His days on the ocean between Key West and Havana were a storehouse of experience that Ernest tended with great care.

Ernest also had luck of another kind that March when Max Perkins came down for his annual fishing vacation. When Max arrived they rented Albert Pinder's large new charterboat, and along with novelist John Herrmann, Chub Weaver, and Burge Saunders, they made for the Tortugas and Ernest's favorite fishing grounds.

Soon after they arrived at the Fort Jefferson docks they ran through their supply of Bermuda onions. When Ernest approached a Cuban crew on board a small fishing smack tied to the dock, he met its captain, a grizzled, sun-lined Canary Islander named Gregorio Fuentes. The cleanliness of the smack impressed Ernest greatly, he later related the incident to Charles Thompson and told him that Fuentes was the kind of man he wanted for a mate should he ever buy a fishing boat himself. The party fished the waters around Tortugas that Ernest regarded as private fishing hole; as usual he had fine luck. Max Perkins left the excursion early, however, due to a business commitment in New York. A fierce storm came in on the Tortugas almost immediately after his departure.

With the storm the luck changed, and the Hemingway party ran low on supplies and completely depleted their supply of ice. In order to save the several hundred pounds of fish they had accumulated by then, Burge and John Herrmann took Bread Pinder's charterboat back the 65 miles to Key West for ice and fresh provisions. Engine trouble delayed them for almost a week. When they finally returned to Tortugas the fish had spoiled, and Ernest was in one of his black rages. The return trip was a strained affair.

Back in Key West after the misadventure in the Tortugas, Ernest "was as restless as a bear," Lorine Thompson observed. Since his slowly healing broken arm would not allow him any serious writing or fishing, he used the injury as a perfect excuse to indulge himself in the sporting pleasures of the city.

By 1931, industry and the Navy had vacated Key West, and gambling—the "other industry," as it was called—was coming into its own in the Keys. Duval Street gambling houses flourished amid a sort of flashing neon halo in the crisp winter air. The Golden Nugget, Delmonico's, the Tradewinds, and Sloppy Joe's all teemed with merchant sailors and tourists who stood in noisy groups around crap tables and "umbrella" (roulette) tables. Blackjack was dealt almost on the narrow sidewalk that fronted Duval Street. Faro tables were crowded, and sailors shot "celo"—three dice—on the barroom floors, while tourists stood mesmerized before "one-arm bandits" waiting for three sets of red cherries to appear in the slot machine windows. "Bolita"—numbers—was thrown locally on a daily basis; "Cuba" was thrown in Havana on Saturday afternoons, and rooster fights were held nightly in the mammoth Cuban Club off Duval Street.

If your luck held in bolita or Cuba you could win $2,000 for a $2 bet, and if you split your bets up among the local bolita bankers you could win as much as $50,000 to $75,000 with a "parley" (1-2-3 digit number combination). Or if you were a "butter-and-egg-money" bettor—as most housewives were—you could bet a nickel with Octavio "Tabby" Cervantes, who was known as the "penny man," and win $5.

Bolita was such a way of life then in Key West that the city was clearly marked off in block territories; routes were "owned" by salesmen who worked for one of the several Cuban families who were "bankers." All the transactions from route salesman to banker were made in cash, and it was not uncommon for a major banker to have $100,000, even

$200,000 in cash in his house. In the tradition of accredited banks, bolita banks and bankers were scrupulously honest. Winning numbers were posted in street corner booths strategically placed all over town for all to see.

On the waterfront artery—Front Street—nothing on the island rivaled the already infamous "Habana Madrid," a rambling combination of indoor and outdoor compartments where the music, dancing, gambling, and fist fights went on twenty four hours a day. The Havana prostitutes who came to Key West once a month for a few days' stay in the rooms in the club's interior were well received by the locals. It was justly said during the 1930s and 1940s that if you couldn't get what you wanted in the Habana Madrid, it hadn't been invented yet. And in 1931, two full years before Prohibition was repealed for the rest of the country, the Florida Keys were as "wet" as the gin-clear waters that surrounded them.

With all this illegal activity going on on the nine-square mile island, the first question that popped into the mind of the tourist or the visitor was "Where are the police?" They were there, and they were honest and hardworking by Key West standards. Key West standards simply allowed gambling. The gambling was strongest among the Cubans who had earlier brought it over from Havana, but all the islanders gambled.

"Damn!" the Cubans said, "You gamble! You gamble!" And to them it was just that simple.

And to the police, a majority of whom were Cuban, it was also that simple. They made raids, of course. After all, gambling was illegal in Florida, and they were forced to admit that they were part of Florida, but the raids were on a token basis at best. As a courtesy the banker or gambling house owner who was to be raided was notified well in advance by a police go-between, the raid was staged, and the gambler or banker taken to police headquarters (then in the old city hall on Greene Street).

At police headquarters the routine called for rough jokes to be exchanged by both parties, and then without a formal or recorded booking taking place, the gambler would be given a small slip of paper on which was marked simply the date he was to appear in city court. In city court the gambler, would be fined, depending on the size and wealth of his operation, and the money would be scrupulously placed in the city treasury, completing a cycle that in essence amounted simply to a city gambling tax.

There was a local joke in those days that if city court was, after a fashion, rigged, the federal courts would not even get a chance at a Key West gambler. And during the heyday of Key West gambling (the 1920s to the 1940s) the federal courts did indeed experience a dry spell with regard to Key West gamblers. The reason why federal law enforcement officers failed to make arrests in Key West was quite uncomplicated. Sitting 120 miles off the mainland and accessible by routes that had what amounted to check points (the FEC train depot, the No Name Key ferry slip, and the P&O and Mallory shipyard terminals) a suspicious mainlander or federal man had no chance of coming into town unannounced. In any event, with the economic damper the Great Depression was putting on the nation, the zeal of federal law enforcement was not at a consistently high pitch.

And if a federal man did come into town, as happened infrequently, the police exercised roughly two choices: arrest him and give him the bum's rush and apologize later, or close down the more obvious gambling houses along Front and Duval Streets. As it happened, one choice was used with about as much regularity as the other.

But the patrons of the Cuban Club, an imposing, rambling, white wood-frame structure on the corner of Amelia and Duval Streets, did not fear either federal or local lawmen. Its high-ceilinged walls offered a sort of temporal sanctuary to the Cubans and Cuban-Americans who were in daily and nightly attendance there around the gambling tables and bars, meeting halls, restaurant, and dance floor. Membership was limited strictly to Cubans or Cuban-Americans, and it was not only a favorite of locals but also of visiting Cuban dignitaries who frequently came over from Havana.

In 1931, Key West was very much under a Cuban influence, and it was totally out of the question for a non-Cuban to even suggest that he be allowed inside for even a quick drink. The Conchs and the members of the local black community had their own gathering places, though none offered the total protection of the Cuban Club. For the Conchs, Raul's and Pena's were favorite spots, and there was an ample number of civic and fraternal organizations that afforded their members clubhouses. The blacks also gathered nightly along Petronia Street in bars that usually bore the names of their owners.

Though they usually frequented separate bars, the three groups of people maintained a familiar harmony. Times had begun to get hard as the Depression wore on, and it was not uncommon to see the mother of a black family walking across the street to the home of her white or Cuban neighbors with a hot bowl of steaming, aromatic food, or vice versa.

In 1931, nothing in Key West rivaled the pleasure of two institutions that have now passed into history: the rooster fights and the finest houses of prostitution in America. There were rooster fights at the Cuban Club, and there were a number of small-time or backyard fights about town, but the big rooster fight was held where Amelia Street came to a dead end in the predominantly black southwestern quarter of the city. Where the street came to a dead end there was a large open lot dotted with short grass and sand spurs; in the center there was a circular, fenced-in area defined by slats and baling wire where the ground was rock hard and bare. On the north and south sides of the circular arena, low bleachers accommodated little more than a hundred spectators.

Promptly at noon on Sunday (much as in the Latin tradition of the bullfight) the rooster trainers and handlers would begin arriving at the arena carrying their fighting charges in brightly colored cages, each marked with the name of the rooster. Cars lined Amelia Street all the way back to its intersection with Emma Street. Within an hour after the first of the fighting roosters had arrived, a noisy crowd of Cubans and Conchs, decked out in Sunday whites, loud ties, and sweat-stained Panama hats had gathered around the arena.

Vendors began circulating among the crowd with home-made popsicles frozen fast to twigs from buttonwood trees. Colorful half-glass, half-wood carts filled with steaming hot tacos were stationed at intervals along narrow Amelia Street. Bottles of strong homemade wine passed from friend to friend among the crowd; here and there a half pint of "Hoover Gold" was uncorked and savored.

Minutes before 1:00 PM the noise of the crowd subsided to a low murmur down from the Emma Street intersection along Amelia Street. It was the unwritten signal that the first bettors had arrived out on Emma Street. The bettors—the wealthiest Cubans on the island (usually the big-time bolita bankers), wealthy Conchs, and some of the reigning political figures of the day—pulled their cars up to the curb on Emma Street. In the true machismo style they descended from their cars and greeted one another cordially but with the reserve and distance that their roles as competitors imposed. Then they walked regally down Amelia Street under the respectful eyes of all.

At 1:00 PM two handlers squared their colorful gamebirds off against one another. This matching had been arranged only minutes before and revolved around the simple and stoic challenge.

"You want to fight your rooster?"

"Yes, I want to fight my rooster."

The birds could be fought with or without razor-sharp artificial talons, but as they had been trained since adulthood to attack—to kill—they immediately went for each other with almost a fanatic zeal. As soon as the trainers released the birds a referee inverted an hour glass that usually held enough sand for a 15- to 30-minute match, and then began two distinct circles of betting: among the bettors in the stands and among the trainers and handlers themselves.

To a layman what transpired after that point was as baffling as calculus is to a first-year math student. Amid an air as sedate as a formal art auction, thousands, on occasion tens of thousands, of dollars began to change hands, and all without a single penny showing in the crowd. The ounce of difference between roosters was quickly erased in odds that were given in proportion to the weight of the lightest rooster.

When a bet was proposed it was accepted by a bettor with the word "pago"—"I take the bet!" If a rooster was downed the trainer rushed to it, and if the bird could continue the trainer released it and shouted "¡va la pelea!"—"the fight goes on." It was said that smart trainers and handlers could always cover their bets to such an extent that no matter how their rooster fared in the ring they could take a thousand to fifteen hundred dollars from the crowd each Sunday.

The outcome of a rooster fight was usually so obvious that explanation and technicalities were unnecessary. A rooster won the fight when his opponent became too weak to continue, either from vicious pecks or spur kicks with heels. Usually the losing rooster died or was killed a short time after the fight. But sometimes they could be expertly patched up, and it was not uncommon to see a rooster with two fights behind him entering the ring with only one eye.

In the rare event that neither bird pecked or kicked the other for the time limit, the event was declared a draw and no money changed hands. But a draw was a disgrace of the first magnitude to the-trainers and handlers, and the uncooperative gladiators had their necks summarily wrung as a result. Rooster fighting was usually the sole occupation of the handlers and trainers; one handler even kept his prize bird in a gold-plated cage under his bed.

The average rooster could stand no more than two or three grueling stretches in the ring. Most retired early into a kitchen pot. By late afternoon the fights had been staged, and the principals repaired to speakeasies or motel rooms to square accounts. It was not uncommon for fortunate bettors to end the day five to ten thousand dollars richer.

But the pleasure, above all other pleasures that the machismo crowd enjoyed in Key West from the turn of the century and in varying degrees until Castro closed down Cuba in 1961 (because Key West, no matter how provincial it appeared on the surface, was always in competition with bawdy, cosmopolitan Havana) was in its houses of prostitution. The two most famous houses of pleasure were the Square Roof on the corner of Emma and Petronia Streets and Mavis Lee's (name changed) on the corner of Howe and Truman Avenue (then Division Street).

The Square Roof was done up in bright colors, some years bright yellow, some years pink. Its specialty was opulent rooms staffed by beautiful black women, some of Bahamian ancestry, some of mixed black and Chinese blood, some of mixed black and Creole, and some of pure African descent. But as this was another age, these lovely, voluptuous, dark-skinned, and flashing-eyed beauties were for the pleasures of only the white man. They enjoyed a special but precarious position. At the same time that they scorned blacks, the prostitutes at the Square Roof alternately admired and disdained the white men who sported them for money.

The Square Roof, run by a petite, light-skinned black woman Naomi Lamberts (name changed), whose chastity was as absolute as her fanatic Catholicism, catered to the rich Cubans and Conchs of the city and to selected visitors they brought or recommended. While it is tempting to report that Ernest Hemingway and his Mob visited this local attraction even that first spring of 1928—after all, they came early under the protection and guidance of Key Westers who certainly had an entree to the establishment—there is no evidence to substantiate the fact.

In his Key West novel, *To Have and Have Not,* parts of which were begun only five years after he arrived in 1928, Hemingway makes reference to Mavis Lee and her establishment according to a confidential source who knew both Hemingway and Mavis Lee.

"Big Lucie's daughter came in with that girl from their place…" and later "That's all they pick on now," says Big Lucie's daughter. "Any kind of sporting people. Anybody with any sort of cheerful outlook."

Later in the same novel, Hemingway makes reference to the wife of Albert Richards who had left the sporting life in the "jungle town" section of the city for marriage, using a technique he often employed of borrowing bits and pieces for different characters from the same real life person—in this instance Mavis Lee.

In *To Have and Have Not,* Hemingway captured the island's live-and-let-live mood ("the Key West Rhythm") as well as it has ever been chronicled. Speaking to an out-of-towner, one of his characters, a laconic old Conch charterboat captain, Captain Willie, says: "Down here everybody aims to mind their own business."

And later in a heated exchange with one of his passengers, after he is ordered to "meddle" in Harry Morgan's (the book's protagonist's) business, and is told that his passenger is "one of the biggest men in [Roosevelt's New Deal] administration," he sums up the total Key West feeling: "Nuts," said Captain Willie. "If he's all that what's he doing in Key West?"

That indeed was the feeling of the Conchs of Key West. They were end-of-the-liners who wanted to be left alone.

In one of his private journals of that period, Hemingway wrote of Key West: "In this town there are people who have never been in any other part of town."

During the early spring of 1931, it was becoming apparent to Pauline and all those who knew Ernest that Key West was the sort of town he meant to settle down in. Pauline still favored a return to Paris or to a villa on the Mediterranean, or even to a residence in suburban Bridgeport, Connecticut.

The possibilities were almost limitless because Uncle Gus Pfeiffer had informed Pauline of his intention to buy them a house when they found an "agreeable location." It was a practice Uncle Gus had established with his relatives and one he greatly enjoyed.

For his part, Uncle Gus preferred Bridgeport, where he already had a sort of compound of Pfeiffers flourishing. But he told Pauline he would not "press the issue" on the matter of where they chose to live, for he added that Ernest's feeling had to be considered greatly. From the start Uncle Gus was a fan not only of Hemingway prose, but of Ernest himself. And that spring (during mid-March), when it became apparent to Pauline that she would have their second child, serious discussions began between them as to where they should settle.

Pauline preferred Europe, but she told Lorine Thompson that she knew from the beginning that "Ernest had his heart set on Key West." So a search was launched during the last days of March 1931 for a suitable home for the Hemingways. With the Great Depression almost two years old there were ample vacant houses in Key West from which to pick. But even after careful inspection by Pauline and Lorine, and on occasion by Ernest himself and Charles Thompson, nothing could be found that met their essential requirements: a secluded place for Ernest to write; ample living and sleeping quarters for Ernest, Pauline, two children, and servants; a yard spacious enough for the privacy she and Ernest required; and a setting with the European flavor Pauline desired.

As the first days of April came in, no house that met the specifications had been found. It was Lorine who finally reminded Pauline that "Well, there's always the haunted house." Almost grudgingly, Pauline decided to take a second look at the ramshackle house where she had gotten an eyeful of plaster the year before.

The lot was sparsely dotted with palm trees, and only a few shrubs were in evidence in the back yard facing Olivia Street. Pauline and Lorine made a second inspection of the property, keeping to the outside at first. As it happened, Uncle Gus Pfeiffer was in town at the time on an invitation from Ernest to go on a fishing excursion to the Dry Tortugas. When he returned, Pauline and Lorine took him around on an inspection tour of the house. It seemed in ill-repair, but it was a very dignified old structure with almost unlimited possibilities.

After Pauline showed an interest, they called on Jerry Trevor, who was then the president of the Florida First National Bank. Lorine had learned from friends that Trevor, through his bank, had lately come into possession of the house. Trevor, an old-line Conch, gave Pauline and Lorine a guided tour of the property and soon after quoted Pauline a price that she conveyed to Uncle Gus. For his part, Ernest retained a disdainful composure throughout the inspection and negotiations, although he maintained from the start that he would not leave Key West—"it had to be Bone Key."

Finally, on April 29, 1931, the negotiations and discussions were completed, and the property was conveyed from "Jerry J. Trevor, President of the Florida National Bank" to "Ernest Miller Hemingway, 4 Place de la Concorde, Paris, France c/o Guaranty Trust Co. of New York City;" that address was the final vestige of their Paris years.

The document was witnessed by Mary F. Whitmarsh (after whose family Whitmarsh Lane was named) and William H. Malone, who was later to be mayor of Key West. The purchase price was $8,000, and it redeemed a succession of mortgage failures. The legal description recorded in the Monroe County Courthouse ceded a piece of property from Trevor to Hemingway defined as "189.4 feet on Whitehead Street, and 197.9 feet on Olivia Street." The house, done in the style of a large Spanish colonial estate—in reality a mansion, although Ernest detested the word—was then almost eighty years old, having been built in 1851 by shipping tycoon Asa Tift (one of the founders of Tifton, Georgia).

The main body of the house was quarried from white coral stones cut on the property from the giant hole that became one of the only basements on the island. Wood for the house—white, ironlike heart of pine—was cut on Tift's land and shipped to the island from Georgia. Two wide iron railing porches encircled both floors. Each side of the house was punctuated by four symmetrically-arched, shuttered windows that stood floor length into the stone walls.

Drinking water was supplied from a 20,000-gallon stone and wood cistern in the rear of the house. In later years, when Key West got city water from the Navy pipeline, the cistern was capped and the huge concrete base was used as a dance floor. Over the years, over Pauline's objections, Ernest furnished the walls and most of the floors with the animal skins and heads he had shot on his various hunting trips.

The $8,000 had been deposited by Uncle Gus from his account at the New York Guaranty and Trust Company to an account for the Hemingways. Ernest celebrated the signing of the deal by getting happily drunk at Sloppy Joe's with Charles Thompson, who remained somewhat sober and drove him home to the rented house on the corner of Whitehead and United Streets, six blocks from the house he now owned. Pauline had drinks that night in Pena's Garden of Roses with Lorine Thompson, in a mood somewhere between gloom and apprehension.

Charles and Lorine Thompson were probably the two happiest people in Key West that night of April 29, 1931; the Hemingways had after all settled seemingly for good on their little island, insuring exciting winter seasons for many years to come. But on April 30, Pauline "horrified me," Lorine later said, by announcing that she and Ernest would not be doing any work on the new house until the following winter. They would be leaving for Spain within the week, she informed

Lorine, so that Ernest could continue his much interrupted bullfight book, *Death in the Afternoon.*

"Besides," Pauline told Lorine, "you have to live in a house for a time before you really know what to do with it."

Considering that the roof leaked and numerous windows were broken and, in general, the old place had, as Pauline had initially noted, the look and feel of a "haunted house," the simple prospect of even living in the house without considerable prior work did not seem plausible to Lorine. But "without so much as lifting a finger" on the new house, Pauline, young Patrick, and his nurse entrained for New York during the first days of May to make connections for Paris. On May 4 Ernest left Havana harbor on board a liner bound for Spain.

In Paris once more, Pauline's first order of business was to retrieve her hoard of fine French and Spanish furniture from storage and have it shipped to the new house in Key West.

After he had situated Pauline, Patrick, and Patrick's nurse in the familiar setting of Hendaye Plage for the summer, Ernest went to Madrid, where in the company of a diverse set of cronies, he made the bullfights from August through October. By November he and his family were back in Kansas City awaiting the birth of their second child. On November 12, 1931, again at the Research Hospital and again by caesarean section, a healthy baby boy named Gregory Hancock Hemingway was born. By early December Pauline had recovered, so much so that she and Ernest and their two sons were back in Piggott by the end of the first week in December to present the new addition to the Pfeiffer clan. During the second week of December Pauline and baby Gregory were pronounced fit enough to travel, and by mid-December 1931, the Hemingways were back in Key West and installed in the new house.

Though Key West had seemed the end of the line three years before, it was now home for the Hemingways. It was winter, and Ernest's Mob would soon be descending once

more. The Gulf Stream flowed at his doorstep, and for diver-
sion there was cosmopolitan Havana only 90 miles away.

Now the myth of Papa could begin. It had been germinat-
ing from almost his first days in the island city in the spring of
1928. Now it was rooted in Key West. For the next eight years
the myth grew, until Ernest's separation from Pauline in
December 1939. By that time the myth was of such stature that
it could be wrapped like a present, carried across the Gulf
Stream, and opened for Christmas in Havana.

3

The Papa Myth Begins

Ernest and Pauline and their two young sons moved into the 907 Whitehead Street house six days before Christmas in 1931. But neither Christmas or the new house occupied the majority of Ernest's thoughts. He was beginning the revision of *Death in the Afternoon*. His first need was a place where he could do his exacting and tedious brand of editing in relative peace while a small army of out-of-work Conchs descended on the house to revamp everything from the antique plumbing and crumbling plaster to rotted window frames, broken windows, and rain-warped doors.

One of the deciding factors in buying the house had been the two-story outbuilding that stood to the rear of its north side. It became known as the poolhouse after Pauline had a massive swimming pool constructed in their backyard in 1937, but now it was simply a dilapidated tool shed and onetime carriage house with neglected servant's quarters on the small and boxlike second floor. But as inglorious as it looked, it received the first attention of the workmen. The plaster cracks were shored up and the room was repainted a light sea green. The floor was of planking then. In 1933, Ernest's friends in Havana shipped him a large number of Cuban tiles—gold, brown, and white. Later, Toby Bruce used them to resurface the poolhouse floor, making it a workroom where Ernest began or finished the bulk of his writings published during his lifetime.

In this poolhouse workroom Ernest completed *Death in the Afternoon,* his collection of short stories entitled *Winner Take Nothing;* his African safari book, *Green Hills of Africa;* his Key West book, *To Have and Have Not;* revisions of his only play, *The Fifth Column;* parts of his Spanish Civil War documentary, *The Spanish Earth;* and, before he left Key West in 1939, the beginning of *For Whom the Bell Tolls.*

He also wrote all or parts of his finest short stories—"The Snows of Kilimanjaro" and "The Short Happy Life of Francis Macomber"—while in Key West.

Initially, Ernest furnished his workroom with a squat cigar-maker's wood-frame chair having a wide leather bottom and a narrow leather back piece, and a simple round table on which he worked out his handwritten manuscript pages. The corners of the room were lined with boxes of old manuscripts and boxes of bits of works-in-progress, together with artifacts from his days as a lieutenant in the Italian Army (his helmet, one of his World War I dress uniforms, and various army belts and buckles).

The entire room was littered with the copious notes he had assembled over the past few years on the spectacle of bull-fighting, as well as several hundred photographs, many of which eventually found a place in the well-illustrated *Death in the Afternoon.* Later Toby Bruce made him an elaborate wall shelf with over 50 manuscript-sized cubbyholes, but for the moment, in 1931, as Christmas drew near, the study resembled something like a "lightly organized waste paper can," Pauline observed to Lorine Thompson.

For her part, Pauline supervised the work on the house as

best she could, but she was still so weak from her caesarean childbirth that she was obliged to sleep in the living room rather than climb the short flight of stairs to the second floor. Her sister Virginia ("Jinny" or "Gin") soon appeared, and with Lorine Thompson she strung bolts of cheesecloth on the ceiling of the children's room on the Olivia Street side of the house. The ceiling was so badly cracked from what later was found to be the main source of the great leaks in the roof that the plaster chipped and fell into the boys' eyes while they lay in their cribs. The cheesecloth worked as a temporary measure in the boys' room, but it seemed—much to Lorine Thompson's disgust—that all Pauline had in mind for the house initially were temporary measures.

"We're just going to have to live here for a while before I know what I'm going to do with the place," Pauline assured Lorine.

"Yes," retorted Lorine, "but you have to first be able to live in a house."

Lorine was convinced that the house was then unlivable, and while the boys' room was in the worst repair, things were not much better in the other six rooms. Ernest was obliged to sleep by himself in an enormous bedroom that with its adjoining bath occupied the entire southwesterly part of the upstairs; he also fell asleep staring at a cracked plaster ceiling. The housekeeper's room on the northwest corner of the second floor was in equally bad shape; its windows would not fully close at first. The massive living room on the southwest side (the right side as you entered from Whitehead Street) of the first floor was littered with packing crates of furniture from Paris and piles of lumber that were being used in the restoration, all forming a wall of confusion around Pauline's sickbed.

The dining room and kitchen on the left side of the first floor served mostly as a storage and work area for the repairmen at first. With Pauline's condition, an infant, a small child, and a house that was in total disarray, there was no thought of formal dinners or entertaining.

What was becoming known as the vibrant Hemingway lifestyle began that Christmas season of 1931, though, and despite Lorine Thompson's general reservations, a Christmas tree was erected at the foot of Pauline's bed.

Only Dos Passos and his wife Kate came into town that winter season, however, and only for a brief stay. Life at the Hemingways revolved around their growing family and old Key West friends like Charles and Lorine Thompson, Joe Russell, Sully Sullivan, and Captain Bra Saunders. This season (December of 1931 and the winter of 1932) was devoted to work on *Death in the Afternoon.*

To complicate matters in mid-December, Patrick, a mischievous lad of almost three, gave baby Gregory a liberal spraying of a toxic potion he mixed in a spray can, then proceeded to eat an ant-repellent pellet that contained a small amount of arsenic, enough to send him into a vomiting spell for the next twenty-four hours.

Patrick's French nurse Gabrielle also became ill, and in the midst of all the confusion Ernest fell sick with a severe sore throat, a malady he could ill afford as he raced to get his rewrite job done on his new book. To further complicate matters as the new year of 1932 came in, Lorine Thompson and Jinny Pfeiffer were forced to turn their efforts from moving furniture to assisting Pauline with the typing of the new manuscript as the first cold snap of the winter brought her to bed. Finally by mid-January, after Lorine Thompson was forced to enlist some of her students to do the typing, Ernest finished rewriting the book and mailed the bulky typescript to New York and Max Perkins.

But he no sooner finished his 150,000-word, richly illustrated book than he went back to his writing desk again, this time to a genre he had not followed for some time: short stories, the prose form of which he is still the undisputed American master. One of the short stories he completed early that winter was "After the Storm," taken from the true story Captain Bra Saunders had told him in 1928 on his first trip to the Dry Tortugas about the sinking of the Spanish liner *Val Banera*. All the short stories he completed that winter, together with several that had already appeared in periodicals, were published by Scribner's in 1933 in a collection entitled *Winner Take Nothing*.

Why Ernest turned so quickly to another writing project— a practice that was not typical of him at that time—is not clearly evident. His right arm had healed fully from the Montana automobile accident and he was telling not only his Key West cronies but writing in letters that his "juices" were "going like mad." He may simply have turned to writing one of the finest collections of stories in self-defense against all the confusion around his house or as a good excuse not to lend a hand.

Whatever the motive, with his writing and shooting arm healed and his juices up from short story production, Ernest gained the impetus to address himself once again to a project of prime importance—his long put-off safari in Africa. It was 1932, however, the worst year of the Great Depression. The trip was supposed to be financed by Uncle Gus Pfeiffer with $25,000 of Richard Hudnut stock. Unfortunately, the stock had dropped sharply and Ernest was again forced to postpone his safari and content himself with fishing in the Dry Tortugas and off Cuba, and with big game hunting out West.

While Ernest's attentions were turned necessarily to literature and his plans for fishing and hunting, Pauline, who by late February had recovered from her caesarean childbirth ordeal, was confronted with the pure, tedious burden of organizing the Hemingway household. The house, a full two months after they moved in, finally was beginning to assume the look and feel of a home. By then the house had been rewired and the plumbing repaired, and the windows and doors had been shaved so that they closed properly. The roof no longer leaked, and the workmen had sealed up the plaster cracks in the walls and ceilings. The sections of warped pine flooring had been replaced by new wood that stuck out markedly in a pale yellow against the aged brown floor panels that had been in place a full fourteen years before the American Civil War began. But to Lorine Thompson's continued dismay, no paint had been applied to the walls or the house.

"You got drunk trying to follow the directions the patches took," she commented about the rather tattered and undignified designs in the plaster patching.

While Pauline had her Paris furniture arranged throughout the house, she still intended to have the Piggott furniture-maker Toby Bruce construct a number of hand-worked wood pieces (including an oversized bed for Ernest and Pauline and a number of ornate end tables and wine racks). She remained firm in not painting the big house until she had achieved the right effect with her combination of furniture. Painting was not Pauline's main problem that first winter in her new home. A staff of servants was an essential requirement. This became all the more pressing when her sister Jinny departed in February; and Patrick's French nurse Gabrielle had not fully recovered from her illness.

With the Depression strangling Key West, it was not difficult to find willing workers, but the task was to find qualified domestic workers. Key Westers were, after all, fishermen or people of the sea, not servants. Ernest dictated that the immediate necessity upon arrival in December was finding a cook the equal of the Thompsons's Bahamian woman, Phoebe. Fortunately Pauline located a Key West black woman named Isabelle soon after Christmas who proved adequate even to Phoebe's high standards. Jimmy Smith, a local black man, a widower in his late thirties with three small children, was hired as a gardener, and a black woman named Ina Hepburn was hired as the washwoman.

Another local black named Bobby was put on the staff as a very informal butler; because he could do a professional-level soft shoe dance, he soon acquired the nickname "Dancing Bobby." He strutted about the house in his white cotton coat like its most important member.

But the real head of the servants was a no-nonsense Yankee woman—the only white member of the household staff—Ada Stern. An authoritative looking woman in her forties, she came to work for the Hemingways that year and ran a disciplined and orderly house for Pauline, who was willing to give over the domestic chores of the house to another. And Ada remained in her role as a live-in housekeeper until Patrick and Gregory left Key West in the late 1940s for out-of-state schools.

But of the staff it was Isabelle, a saucy black woman, buxom, in her prime, who gave both Ada and Pauline what Lorine Thompson described as the standard "run for their money" that winter.

Although Pauline had run afoul of the Catholic Church with her marriage to Ernest, she nevertheless remained a staunch Catholic with a strong disdain for adultery. Isabelle, for her part, summed up marriage with a blatant "My husband, he's a single man!" Lorine was less traditional in her appraisal of Isabelle's careless attitude to marriage when she said later that "She [Isabelle] always had a husband, sometimes two or three. The trouble was she didn't bother to divorce the old ones!"

Pauline attended to at least one divorce, though, and paid George Brooks, then the Monroe County State Attorney, $50 to divest Isabelle of what presumably was her first husband.

Ernest for his part sided somewhat with Isabelle.

"I don't give a good damn if she's married to everybody in jungle town [the slang name of the predominantly black southwest section of the city] so long as she keeps on cooking good grub," he told Charles Thompson.

By February Ernest abandoned his short story writing temporarily, and, with Captain Bra Saunders and Charles Thompson, he fished the waters around the Dry Tortugas for over a

week. In No-Man's Land—the rough-water area between Dry
Tortugas and the Marquesas Keys—they got into a school of
kingfish and boated enough to pay for the trip. Later in the
week Ernest landed a five-and-a-half foot barracuda from the
rickety wooden Fort Jefferson docks while a surprise north-
wester kicked up three to four foot seas.

"The water was so white-capped it looked like snow,"
Charles Thompson mused later.

The weather, as it so often did, forced the three back to Key
West, but when warm southwest winds came in over calm seas
during the first days of March, Ernest had again assembled his
two fishing companions and they were off to the Tortugas.
Fishing was good on that second trip, but mostly the catch was
of the panfish variety.

"Captain Bra cooked up a pigeon-yellowtail stew that
would have put the best restaurant in Key West out of business," Charles Thompson said. And they washed the creation
down with several green bottles of hock.

For all his fishing delights, and they were considerable,
Ernest had not boated a marlin. Although Hemingway is
linked with the giant billfish, in 1932 the marlin was not the
major big game fish, but rather a beast to be taken by commercial fishermen. The major fishing tackle manufacturers were
only then beginning to cope with the problems of developing
reels to stand the stress of boating monsters 500 pounds and
larger.

In April, Ernest finally got his chance at marlin-hunting, as
it was called then, because the early methods amounted to no
less than stalking them in the Gulf Stream. Joe Russell, the
owner of the Front Street speakeasy, and the rum-running
charterboat captain, regaled Ernest with stories of the giant
fish over drinks in the afternoon. During the first days of April
they journeyed to Cuba in Joe's charterboat, the *Anita*. Joe
charged his old friend only half the usual fee of $20 and they
went as comrades, not as client and captain.

In comparison to the expedition he and Joe made to the same fishing grounds the following year, their first marlin hunting was disappointing. Having no frame of reference for the monster sport, however, Ernest was simply "delighted" with the whole spectacle. Although he and Joe had planned to stay for only two weeks, the fishing was exciting and the Havana nightlife always rivaled Paris, Tangiers, and Munich with its gamey atmosphere, so they dragged the trip out for over two months. And Joe Russell, who never drank at home in Key West, felt very "wet" that spring, he later confided to Charles Thompson.

Pauline came over twice during the protracted stay and found Ernest in good spirits, fishing and working well on the proofs of *Death in the Afternoon* in his second-story room at the Ambos Mundos Hotel on Obispo Street.

Before they returned to Key West aboard the *Anita,* Ernest not only was reading galley proofs on *Death in the Afternoon,* but had completed several more short stories and had boated almost thirty creditable marlin. His fishing advisor was Carlos Gutiérrez, then 53 years old, was the Cuban fisherman Ernest had first met in the Dry Tortugas in 1928. Carlos also would advise Ernest and Joe Russell the following year when they made near-record catches. In 1934 when Ernest bought his Wheeler Shipyard-built yacht *Pilar,* Carlos would serve as its first mate.

In mid-June Ernest and Joe Russell crossed the 90 miles from Havana to Key West in the *Anita,* but almost immediately on his return Ernest fell ill with a minor case of bronchial pneumonia and was confined to his upstairs bedroom. And his considerable discomfort of having a respiratory ailment in the torrid June heat and humidity was compounded when he was once again obliged to return to correcting the galleys of *Death in the Afternoon.*

"In no small way," Lorine Thompson said later, "Pauline kept Ernest's nose to the grindstone. She kept him from going off on the tangents he was sometimes prone to stray into." So when Joe Russell sent word to Ernest by an errand boy to "get your big ass out of bed" so they could return to Cuba for a long weekend of marlin fishing, only his pneumonia kept him away.

With Ernest reasonably in check correcting the galleys of *Death in the Afternoon,* Pauline began taking long walks down Whitehead Street, pushing baby Gregory in his Cuban wicker stroller while Ada Stern kept an active and inquisitive Patrick in tow. A friendly, open person by nature, Pauline could occasionally be stuffy, but she displayed nothing but friendship and compassion to her neighbors who were riding out some of the rockiest days of the Depression on a diet of "grits and grunts."

The Hemingways' immediate neighbors on Whitehead and Olivia Streets and on quaint little Shavers Lane that jutted off from Olivia Street were quiet people of modest means. Otto Kerchiner, a German immigrant, lived in a small wood-frame Conch house next to the Hemingways on Whitehead Street. Mrs. Arthur Shepard, a widow, lived across from the Hemingways on the corner of Olivia Street and the dead-end intersection with Whitehead Street. A Cuban family lived near Mrs. Shepard. On Shavers Lane Miss Marie Chappick, then a middle-aged spinster who was to later write a warm and personal history of Key West, "The Key West Story," lived in the first house on the left off Olivia Street. Ina Hepburn, their washwoman, also lived on Shavers Lane in a small Conch cottage with a sagging front porch, occupying the first house on the right, directly across from Mrs. Chappick's Conch house.

In the early days the other side of Whitehead Street was vacant except for the lighthouse and keeper's house that stood on the corner of Whitehead and Division street (now Truman Avenue). After 1945 the government erected low cost housing and apartments for black families but always—especially after the stone wall was built around the house at 907—the Hemingway house had the distinct air of an oasis in a desert of lesser dwellings.

Pauline disbanded the staff during the last week in June, leaving Ernest in the care of his teen-aged sister Carol, with Isabelle to do the cooking. Since most of the help was paid the top wage of $5 per week plus "extras"—food, old clothes, and bonus money from Ernest—they were sure to be waiting for their old jobs when the Hemingways returned in the fall. Pauline entrained for Piggott with Gregory, Patrick, and Ada Stern.

In early July, Ernest, nearing the end of the work on the proofs of his bullfight book and finally winning his bout with pneumonia, drove out of Key West with Carol for Piggott and then Wyoming for a summer and fall again at the Nordquist Ranch. Charles Thompson was to come out in September for big game hunting in the mountains; he eagerly awaited Indian summer, both his and Ernest's favorite time of the year.

The black gardener, Jimmy Smith, and his three children were installed in makeshift quarters in the bottom half of the poolhouse. He was given an ancient German Luger (that he had absolutely no idea how to use or, for that matter, any intention of using). "Guard the joint with your skin; but only if worse comes to worst," Ernest told him. Jimmy responded by moving in and sleeping a full twelve hours a day, getting his gardening chores in between naps.

Carol Hemingway left Piggott almost immediately and rode the train back to her home in Oak Park, Illinois, where her mother and younger brother Leicester still lived.

After a short visit with the Pfeiffers in Piggott, Ernest and Pauline left their sons behind with Ada Stern and drove west to the Nordquist Ranch near Yellowstone National Park. Pauline later told Lorine Thompson that it was like a "second honeymoon all over again." She had completely recovered from her ordeal with Gregory; Ernest was content and jovial as he neared the end of *Death in the Afternoon;* the plains of Nebraska and Wyoming were alive with good green crops; and the mountains of Wyoming held a strong summer pine freshness. They had picnics along the way, lay in the shade of tall pine trees, and drank wine. Pauline was trim and had had her hair bobbed again as it had been when they first met in Paris years ago. Ernest was big and muscular, heavily tanned from marlin fishing, and handsomely dressed in plaid shirts and Levi's. It was a fine and memorable trip, Pauline wrote Lorine Thompson.

After spending time in Key West the year before, Lawrence and Olive Nordquist greeted Ernest and Pauline like old friends. Ernest and Pauline continued their second honeymoon at the ranch in their rustic log cabin, but once there Ernest began his usual mountain routine of trout fishing and writing. The honeymoon was squeezed in between times, Pauline later told Lorine Thompson. Finally, four days after his thirty-third birthday, Ernest was able to devote his full time to Pauline, trout fishing, hikes, wine picnics, and horseback riding, when he finished and shipped Max Perkins the last batch of galleys of *Death in the Afternoon*. He had wanted to finish the bullfight book on his birthday, but early morning trout fishing and an all night beer bust "got in the way."

Charles Thompson made his first western trip in the second week of September. He was full of excitement and expectation, knowing all the while that the trip was only a prelude to the African safari that was then all but definite for the following year. Unlike Ernest's and Pauline's trip during the summer, America was now a panorama of colors—Indian summer colors—as Charles's train sped through Kansas City and up into the Colorado highlands with the Rockies off in the west, high, serene, and snowcapped. The gentle groves of aspen at waterholes around Cody, Wyoming, framed by the Wapati Mountain Range, were ablaze with early fall colors of yellow, red, orange, and brown.

Ernest met Charles decked out like a native: leather vest, plaid wool shirt, Levi's, boots, and a huge felt cowboy hat that he described as a "Stein and Stein 9-1/2 gallon job." Charles was bundled up in a heavy tweed coat and hunting trousers. They greeted each other warmly.

"Ernest had raised a full beard; he looked like one of the Forty-Niners," he said later.

Once they had Charles's gear and his guns stacked in Ernest's car, they headed northwest out of Cody to the Clark Fork country. Ernest produced a pint of bootleg Canadian whiskey from under the front seat. They toasted Charles's arrival. The trip got off to a fine start.

It was horn season; mountain goat, sheep, moose, antelope, elk, and deer were fair game. Once in camp at the Nordquist Ranch, Ernest allowed Charles only one day to adjust to the mile-high altitude and to rest from the arduous four-day train trip before they packed for a four-day excursion on horseback into the Pilot Creek wilderness section. Although Charles was mightily impressed with the rugged Wyoming back-country terrain, he admitted that their first four days in the field were a "total blank."

Pauline accompanied them on that first trip, but she was apprehensive about leaving baby Gregory for so long a time (she had been away from the infant then for a full two months) and left on September 22 for Piggott. On their second hunting trip, this time in the Timber Creek section out from the Nordquist Ranch, both men bagged large elks. Ernest also potted a coyote and incurred Charles Thompson's silent ire when he shot an eagle on the wing. Charles was also silently put out several nights after the second hunt. Ernest—for no apparent reason other than an overdose of bootleg whiskey—told him and Chub Weaver, the L-Bar-T ranch hand who had driven Ernest's wrecked Ford to Key West after the Montana accident, that he would kill himself "if it came to that." The possibility of his vibrant, vital friend's killing himself shook Charles Thompson. Ernest was prone to make similar shocking statements to see how they would lay with whatever audience he had at the time.

While at the ranch Ernest read the reviews of *Death in the Afternoon,* which Scribner's published in early October. The early reviews were mixed, although Max Perkins was satisfied. But Ernest was more sensitive. Criticism of his book impinged on the macho spectacle itself and on him personally. He was also aware that he was an American outsider, writing about a phenomenon totally Latin, and it was important that his book be respected by his fellow Americans as a basis for Latin acceptance.

Ernest's spirits were livened, though, because by mid-October both he and Charles Thompson had themselves nice-sized grizzly bears that were immediately shipped to a taxidermist for processing into handsome rugs. Before they left during the third week in October, Charles also bagged a bull elk and two buck deer that stocked the Nordquists's smokehouse for a good part of the hard winter that was closing in on them. After a serious last night of drinking and feasting on Charles's newly slain deer, he and Ernest departed Wyoming for the 70 degree sun of Key West on October 16 in a driving snowstorm.

Pauline threw a "whale of a party," Charles Thompson remembered, as he and Ernest lumbered into Key West after the arduous trip through a nation that was "part snow, part undecided, and part sunshine."

The staff of servants had once again assembled. Isabelle, the cook, prepared green turtle steak, black beans, and yellow rice, one of Ernest's favorites; and the whole meal was helped along by several bottles of good French wine—"A cut above the stuff with the toenails still in it," Ernest proclaimed—that he bought in Miami on the way home.

"Dancing Bobby" did his soft shoe to the amusement of all, and Ernest got a statement of condition from Jimmy Smith, as he handed over the rusted Luger.

"All right Old Sack," he said, "anybody storm the battlements while the army was on the summer offensive?"

Jimmy pondered the question for a few moments; finally he answered. "No sir," he smiled, about to confuse military technology in a vague way with meteorology, "the weather it ain't kicked up no storms nor nothing else while you was away."

The dinner table broke up in laughter, but Ernest calmed it down by saying, "Good. A sound unmolested defensive position is what every good commander desires most."

Jimmy pondered the reply, which made no more sense to him than the original question, then told his employer, "You right about that Mr. Hem-n-way. You shore right about that."

He retreated then, smiling, and once he had left, Ernest said, "Best kind of soldier any outfit could want. Stay and fight to the end and not give a damn about the cause. just the fight."

Patrick and Gregory were still in Piggott with their grandparents and Ada Stern, but Ernest's nine-year-old son "Bumby" was with him on a holiday. Pauline soon left Whitehead Street—still with no paint on the walls of their new house—when she received news from Piggott that the boys were ill with whooping cough.

Meanwhile, Key West was not a pleasant place for Ernest, with intermittent squalls of bad weather, his wife gone, and batches of "bloody-assed" reviews of *Death in the Afternoon* arriving almost daily from Max Perkins. To compound all his problems, *A Farewell to Arms* had been made into a movie with a happy ending and was about to be world-premiered in what Hollywood press agents were calling "Hemingway's hometown of Piggott, Arkansas."

Ernest drove John to Piggott in time for Thanksgiving but skipped the premiere and went duck hunting. The stay in Piggott dragged on past Christmas into the new year 1933; by mid-January Ernest, Pauline, Ernest's three sons, and their nurse were all back in Key West.

The first person Ernest looked up when he returned to Key West that winter was Joe Russell. The repeal of Prohibition had already been submitted to the various states in December;

ratification and passage of the twenty-first amendment was less than a month away. Sloppy Joe wanted to return to Cuba for another stint of marlin fishing before he established a legitimate bar in Key West with his rum-running money.

Joe Russell was much on Ernest's mind then anyway; soon after he returned home he began the first of his Harry Morgan stories that more than four years later would be published by Scribner's under the title *To Have and Have Not.* Sloppy Joe and the fictional charterboat captain "Harry Morgan" fused; later, as the short stories centering around Morgan grew, Joe Russell also fused with "Freddy," the fictional bartender of the novel that would be set in Key West, Cuba, and the 90 miles of Gulf Stream in between.

After several business trips in and out of Key West, Ernest and Joe Russell left for Cuba during the early days of April, with Ernest prepared to pay for the trip with articles he had contracted for on one of his New York visits. Arnold Gingrich, a New York publisher, was putting together a men's magazine, and he had contracted with Ernest to produce a series of articles in the form of "letters" for a price of $250 each.

In his first "letter" for the infant *Esquire Magazine* of Autumn 1933, Ernest recalled vividly that second marlin expedition, Joe's boat, its captain, crew, the sights and sounds of Havana and of Cuba itself, and especially of the Stream.

As always the full situation interested Ernest; although his "letter" for *Esquire* was somewhat technical on the subject of marlin fishing, he still displayed his capacity for relating the whole scope of the event.

Finally, his *Esquire* piece may be regarded as his first attempt at personal legend-building. Retrospect does not discredit author, content, or intention. It is what later became known as "pure Hemingway."

Ernest and Joe Russell stayed in Cuba for two full months; by the time they returned to Key West on July 20, one day before Ernest's thirty-fourth birthday, Ernest had finished his collection of short stories for *Winner Take Nothing*. Back in Key West his first chore was to pound out the "Cuban letter" on his marlin fishing exploits for *Esquire*. The sights and sounds of the marlin hunt: the giant fish stealing the bait, running with it, diving, only to rise again in a white crash from the azure water, and then the fight; the incredible struggle between the fisherman and the fish had literally become a part of him.

He filled Charles Thompson, Sully Sullivan, and George Brooks with an endless succession of stories about the adventures over drinks in his shaded backyard at number 907, and he told Charles that he "meant to have" his own boat to chase the big fish in the very near future. He would have his own boat, in less than a year, but now his thoughts turned to his long-deferred African safari. The two months on the Stream off Cuba had eaten into his preparation time, and now his August 7th sailing date for Europe and the first leg of the trip was less than two weeks away.

Ernest was busy; one of the light moments came when the bearskin trophy finally arrived from the West. Ernest displayed the fine rug, complete with its fierce wide open mouth with fanglike teeth, in the upstairs hallway at the head of the stairs. The first morning after the rug was installed in the hall, Isabelle, the cook, taking Ernest and Pauline their breakfast, burst into their room in genuine fright, fleeing from the rug.

"That bear—that bear, he growled at me," she explained to a laughing Ernest and Pauline.

Charles Thompson alone remained on what Ernest somewhat bitterly labeled his "active list" of eligibles for the trip to Africa. Uncle Gus Pfeiffer's Hudnut stock did indeed rally in the slight stock market recovery of 1933, and he generously underwrote the trip with the $25,000 proceeds. The summer fishing season was booming, however, and Charles was forced to remain in Key West to tend his hardware and tackle business until the fall slack season set in on the island.

With only Charles and Ernest definitely making the trip,

Pauline, who had originally planned to visit her sister Jinny in New York or possibly go to Paris for the fall, decided to become the third member of the party. After first "bucking like a mule," as Lorine Thompson observed, Ernest cheerfully gave in and declared that it would be a note of genuine refinement to have a "Memsahib" on safari.

Ernest and Pauline would be gone from their children and their house in Key West for almost nine months; their logistics were no less than those of an army on a summer offensive. Ernest's younger sister Ursula came down from Oak Park to stay with Patrick and Gregory. The full complement of servants stayed on: Isabelle, Dancing Bobby, Jimmy Smith, and Ina Hepburn, with Ursula and Ada Stern running the household, and Lorine Thompson acting in an advisory capacity to the entire household.

In August, just before leaving for Europe, Ernest, Pauline, and her sister Jinny (who would accompany them to Paris, then return to the States) took a short trip to Havana as Cuban revolutionaries and Carlos Manuel de Céspedes deposed the Cuban dictator Gerardo Machado.

In Paris, while they waited for Charles Thompson that late summer and early fall, Jinny and Pauline established themselves in a good hotel and toured Paris and the surrounding countryside; Ernest, with another diverse set of cohorts, made the bullfight circuit in Spain. All the while Ernest shot back last minute letters and memos to Charles in Key West. Charles had long since been delegated to bring Ernest's guns to Paris. Originally Ernest planned to take a 30.06 Mauser, a 6.5 Mannlicher, and a 12-gauge shotgun. Now word came back to Charles to go to his bedroom at 907 Whitehead Street and "round up" Ernest's .38 caliber pistol. Ernest also detailed lists of books he wanted from his workroom, and gave Charles continued advice on what type of clothing to bring. The letters were also richly decorated with news of Paris and the Spanish bullfight towns.

In early November Charles entrained from Key West for New York City, went by steamer to Marseilles, then by train up through the center of France to Paris and a reunion with Ernest and Pauline. Ernest showed up at the train station wearing a black Basque beret and a brown suit and tie with a magnum bottle of champagne clutched tightly in his left hand. He and Charles had a warm reunion and uncorked the champagne immediately after they were settled into their taxi; they even gave the driver a drink, Charles recalled. And then they proceeded on a grand tour of the city on both sides of the Seine from Montreuil to Clichy.

The champagne tour of Paris was typical of the treatment Charles received from the moment he arrived. Ernest took great delight in showing Charles the "rough joints" of his youth. In retrospect, Charles was treated to nothing less than a trial run of *A Moveable Feast,* a book that would not be written for almost 30 years. Before they sailed for Africa on November 22, Ernest and Charles went deer and pheasant shooting from Paris; on their last night in Paris, Ernest, Pauline, and Charles played host to author James Joyce and his wife Nora. Charles found Joyce, then at work on *Finnegans Wake,* "a grand little man."

On November 22, Ernest, Pauline, and Charles Thompson entrained from Paris for Marseilles in time to make a noon connection on the S.S. *General Metzinger.* They skirted Corsica and Sardinia, coming close to Tunis, and then went on straight across the Libyan and Egyptian coast to the entrance to the Suez Canal at Port Said. Cold rain beat down on their ship, but Ernest and Charles boxed in the *Metzinger's* gym and refreshed themselves at its small bar. In Port Said they went ashore, had a good meal in one of the port restaurants, then took an escorted tour of a city, which Charles found "evil, and smelly, but fascinating."

On the second day of December, they had passed Obock, French Somali, at the end of the Red Sea, and entered the Gulf of Aden. They rounded the northeast corner of the Somali Republic and were in Mombasa, Kenya, six days later. When they walked ashore at Mombasa in the sweltering fall heat of East Africa, Ernest wore a brown felt, wide-brimmed Stetson businessman's hat with a dark band that no one had seen him wear before. With the hat set squarely on his head and the sleeves of his white shirt rolled to the elbows, he stepped onto Kenya's soil to begin his momentous hunt. Pauline trailed behind in an ankle-length white dress, gloves, and a ruffled white parasol. Charles brought up the rear in a suit and tie, bareheaded, and "burning up."

"Pauline and I looked like missionaries," Charles said "while Ernest had the distinct look of a whiskey drummer."

After they cleared customs, the trio adjourned to the nearest bar—a dingy waterfront dive run by two Turks and had German beers and shots of scotch to dedicate the two months of hunting that lay ahead. For a weekend they lingered in the port city of Mombasa and then took the train for the capital city of Nairobi, 300 miles to the northwest. The journey by train took them from the lowland coast of Kenya into the first of the country's highlands, with 17,058 foot Mount Kenya to the east, and 19,340 Mount Kilimanjaro to the west.

Ernest paced up and down their railroad car, exuberant, uncontainable, unable to hide his overflowing emotions behind a sheepish grin that, so Charles Thompson thought, "seemed plastered on his face." He and Charles drank several bottles of French wine they had bought in Mombasa before leaving and at evening when they checked into their comfortable and modern rooms at the New Stanley Hotel, the drinking and merrymaking continued until the early morning hours. The next day all three signed a card and posted it to Lorine Thompson, who was hard at work at her desk in Key West High School. She showed the card to her principal and he told her she should have gone.

"I've got five classes of children to teach," Lorine replied.

"I don't have time to go tramping all over Africa." But in the end she was persuaded to meet them at the end of the hunt in the Holy Land.

Philip Percival, one of Africa's most famous huntsmen, had been contracted as their white hunter. But he was engaged with another party when Ernest, Pauline, and Charles arrived, so they were put up at his Potha Hill farm in Machakos, twenty miles southwest of the capital city near Ngong. Percival and Ernest forged an instant lasting friendship—comparable to those that linked Hemingway with Charles Thompson, Toby Bruce, Captain Eddie Bra Saunders, Charles Scribner, Sr., Winston Guest, Gary Cooper, Colonel Buck Lanham, Taylor Williams, and Antonio Ordonez.

Ernest had learned fishing from Captain Bra and Charles Thompson; he would later learn western big game hunting from Taylor Williams in Sun Valley; now he would learn big game hunting from the greatest white hunter in the world.

From the beginning Pauline was clearly a participant, more or less along for the ride. Ernest and Charles were not engaged in open competition, but any sporting outing with Ernest was always highly competitive. Just as when they had first fished in Key West, Charles had the edge at first. He was simply a better distance shot than Ernest (although Ernest always excelled at close-in wing shooting), and always the condition of Ernest's eyes had to be taken into account. He was terribly nearsighted, but as he had done in the past, Ernest fought back after Charles's early victories in the field and they came out of the hunt on an almost equal footing.

Initially they hunted the Kapiti Plains out from Percival's farm, and for over two weeks they felt their way into African hunting, shooting gazelles that they used for meat and impala that they mounted as heads, plus had some "royal shoots" after guinea fowl.

Tanganyika and the massive and bountiful Serengeti Plain beckoned them. Five days before Christmas, their warm-up

hunting behind them, Ernest, Pauline, and Charles, with
Percival, another white man, Ben Fourie, and a sizable native
contingent set out south from Nairobi on the Cape-to-Cairo
Road for Arusha, 200 miles away, in a convoy of two lorries
and a specially constructed passenger vehicle that was open on
three sides. They spent the night at the Athenaeum Hotel in
Arusha and then pushed on from the northwestern corner of
the Masai steppe in the lowland trough between Lake Eyasi to
the north and Lake Manyara to the south to the eastern edge of
the Serengeti near Shinyanga and Mkalama.

They celebrated Christmas Day in camp near the southwestern end of Lake Eyasi and feasted on gazelle; already
Ernest and Charles had taken an excellent pair of leopards as
well as several other horned beasts. But before the hunt was
two weeks old, as the new year of 1934 came in, Ernest fell ill
with amoebic dysentery. Finally in mid-January Ernest suc-
cumbed to the dysentery when they were camped near the village of Shanwa, near the western end of the great plain.

In a weakened condition Ernest was flown in a small two-
seat rescue plane back to Nairobi, where he convalesced at the
New Stanley Hotel while a doctor filled him with emetine
injections. After little more than a week in bed at the New
Stanley, Ernest rejoined his party, and without rest they pushed
back toward Arusha to the hilly country between Oldeant to
the north and Babati to the south on the edge of the Masai
steppe.

Once in the hills, after having taken lion and plains beast in
the Serengeti, Ernest and Charles took on the more demanding
sport of hunting the greater kudu, sable, and the deadly and
unpredictable rhinoceros. When he returned to his party on the
great plain, Charles Thompson was ahead in game brought
down. Charles too was aware of this, and it made him feel
"uneasy" to be out-shooting his host and friend. Charles,
always easygoing and good natured, did not have to win, he
simply *was* winning.

Back with his safari once more, Ernest intensified his efforts to come off the hunt as champ. But although he got very creditable sized rhino and kudu, Charles always came back to camp with larger specimens.

In early February they broke camp, came out of the hills, and reestablished themselves on the Masai steppe near the village of Babati. Largely at Ernest's insistence they soon moved on south across the steppe to bull kudu country near the village of Kijungu. But the change in locations did Ernest's luck no good. Charles Thompson bagged the first bull kudu, a small one, but a bull. For a few brief days near the end of the hunt Ernest had the illusion that he had bested Charles Thompson when he shot two giant kudu bulls at a salt lick near the Masai village of Kibaya.

But when he returned to camp, Charles, Pauline, and Philip were nervously standing around one of the largest kudu heads ever taken in East Africa. The trophy was Charles's, but he showed little if any pride of ownership. Always good-natured and easygoing, to him it seemed only right and proper that Ernest should get the biggest trophies; but when that did not happen he felt embarrassment rather than pride.

Finally, after two months in Africa, the safari came to an end, and the party repaired to the coast town of Tanga in northeast Tanganyika and then drove north to the Kenya port city of Malindi on the Indian Ocean at the southern end of Formosa Bay. But as the hunt ended, Ernest and Charles managed to get in a few days shooting with Philip Percival's partner, the eccentric and legendary Baron Von Blixen, near Lushoto, in the foothills of a small mountain range near the coast.

"Blixie," as Ernest and Charles called him, was a sawed-off, stern-faced nobleman who at times presented an almost clownlike appearance in his habitual costume of a knee-length bush duster and a weather-beaten, wide-brimmed safari hat. He and Ernest took an instant liking to each other, and Blixie was much impressed with Charles's trophies.

The sting of losing the hunt still churned silently in Ernest just below the surface of his emotions, and he at once engineered a plan to regain some of his steam. He established Pauline in the plush Palm Beach Hotel in Malindi then hastily put together a deep-sea fishing trip with the white hunter Philip Percival as his guest. At the Palm Beach, Ernest and Charles had struck up an acquaintance with a youthful and wiry-haired Alfred Vanderbilt. Vanderbilt, a young man in his twenties, was finishing his own safari, and when Ernest broached the subject of deep-sea fishing along the Indian Ocean coast from the island of Pemba to Zanzibar, Alfred thought it was a "regal suggestion."

"He paid half the expenses," Charles Thompson said. "We all knew he was worth millions, but to hear him talk, and to see him, you wouldn't think he had a dime. He was as pleasant as could be."

Ernest chartered an ancient scow sight unseen, but the vessel proved to have one engine that was "useless" and another that was "worthless." Under these conditions the party constructed makeshift fighting chairs on the stern of the boat and chugged and bumped along the central African coastline after dolphin, kingfish, sails, and panfish such as grouper and jacks. The fishing excursion was in every way anticlimactic; no giant tuna or marlin appeared for Ernest to redeem himself. Even the sailfish were of average size, but his exuberance with Africa in general more than compensated him, and the safari ended in early March on a note of harmony, with Ernest, true to his nature, already planning ways to return.

Coming back might not be an impossibility. While he had been in Africa, Max Perkins had written that *Winner Take Nothing* was selling over the 12,000 mark, and *Cosmopolitan Magazine* had cabled an offer of $5,500 for Ernest's "Harry Morgan" short story that would eventually find its way into *To Have and Have Not.*

Lorine Thompson took leave of her classroom in Key West

and came by freighter from New York to Haifa, Palestine, to meet Ernest, Pauline, and Charles when they arrived on the *Gripsholm* during the first week in March. When her freighter docked in Beirut, many of the passengers elected to rent a car and rejoin the cruise in Haifa, but Lorine chose to remain on board and as a consequence arrived in the Palestinean seaport several days before the *Gripsholm* docked. Once in Hafia, Lorine Thompson, quite obviously alone but eager to see the sights, was taken in tow by an International Harvester salesman who got her a quaint little room at a pension called the Windsor.

When she finally met the *Gripsholm* several days later, she had a good reunion with Charles and then produced snapshots of Patrick and Gregory for Ernest and Pauline to see. Pauline was almost moved to tears at seeing the photographs of the children.

"Poor little lambs," she said. "I can see they miss Mummy."

Lorine immediately moved out of the Windsor and into spacious quarters with Charles on the *Gripsholm.*

The following day the four hired a car and drove to Jerusalem and had a wine picnic in a pleasant little olive grove on the banks of the Sea of Galilee. While they were relaxing after the lunch, Charles observed that the sea was so calm that he almost thought he could walk on it. "Wouldn't prove a thing," Ernest offered good-naturedly, "it's been done before."

On the voyage back to France, the four disembarked in Villefranche and hired a car and drove to Monte Carlo and had lunch at the casino without gambling.

"Ernest took one look at the place," Lorine observed, "and said he felt he had about as much chance winning any money there as he would if he bet on snowstorms in his backyard in Key West."

From Monte Carlo they returned by hired car to Nice, from there entrained for France, and by mid-March they were in Paris, established in comfortable rooms at the Paris-Dinard in the Rue Cassette. After Lorine Thompson had been given a suitable whirl around Paris, she and Charles left for New York and Key West.

Ernest and Pauline stayed in Paris almost two weeks, seeing James Joyce and Sylvia Beach. They returned to America on the *Ile de France*. When the *Ile* docked in New York in April, Ernest put the capper on what he told Charles had been "the greatest adventure" of his life. With $3,000 in advances for magazine articles he would soon write for *Esquire Magazine,* Ernest placed the down payment on a 38-foot power yacht that he had specially built at the Wheeler Shipyard, City Island, New York. The total price was $7,455, and with all his current plans for writing, he was sure he could make up the balance in no time at all. He would name the craft *Pilar.* It would be a sleek, black-hulled vision of grace in the water, trimmed out in brilliant mahogany, and it would occupy most of Ernest's free time for the rest of his life.

He and Pauline took the train back to Key West, and he tried to be patient and wait out the thirty days for the boat to be completed and sailed to Miami. When Ernest returned to Key West in the spring of 1934, he had no way of knowing that the essential trappings for the Papa Myth were almost all in place. He was a teen-aged war hero, a newspaperman, a foreign correspondent, a recognized authority on bullfighting, an author of seven books, an accomplished world traveler, a fisherman, and big-game hunter. Now on a small dot of land in Long Island Sound workmen were constructing for him what became the major component of the myth. He awaited delivery, Pauline noted, "with all the reserve of a small boy waiting at the mailbox for a birthday present."

4

Pilar

To describe *Pilar* as simply a fishing yacht, an impersonal piece of machinery used in the taking of fish, is to do both it and its owner a supreme disservice. *Pilar* became an extension of Hemingway's personality, and it continued to facilitate the growth of that personality and the habits that evolved from it until only months before his death in 1961. And that personality made full use of the opportunity that the *Pilar* afforded, to extend the writer's heroic stature. *Pilar* was the right tool for Ernest and his Papa Myth that now, in 1934, was growing rapidly.

Fifteen years after he acquired the *Pilar*, after it had become as much a part of him as his writing, he could look at it objectively as a piece of hardware:

> *Pilar* was built to be a fishing machine—that would be
> a good sea boat in the heaviest kind of weather, have a
> minimum cruising range of five hundred miles, and sleep
> seven people. She carries three hundred gallons of gaso-

line in her tanks and one hundred and fifty gallons of water. On a long trip she can carry another hundred gallons of gas in small drums in her forward cockpit and the same extra amount of water in demijohns. She carries, when loaded full, 2,400 pounds of ice.

Wheeler Shipyard, of New York, built her hull and modified it to our specifications, and we have made various changes in her since. She is a really sturdy boat, sweet in any kind of sea, and she has a very low-cut stern with a large wooden roller to bring big fish over. The flying bridge is so sturdy and so reinforced below you can fight fish from the top of the house.

Holiday, July 1949

Ernest was in the midst of what was by then an habitual gathering at his house when word reached him on May 9, 1934, that the *Pilar* had arrived in Miami by rail. Gerald and Sara Murphy, friends from the Paris days, Dos Passos and his wife Kate, and Ada MacLeish, as well as Charles and Lorine Thompson were all in attendance for the almost nightly feasts at either Ernest's or at Charles's home on Fleming Street. A genuine party mood accompanied the news of the yacht's arrival. Ernest's nineteen-year-old brother Leicester, nicknamed the "Baron," along with a youthful companion from Petosky, Michigan, named Al Dudek, were also in town. Les and Dudek had just arrived after sailing across the Gulf of Mexico from the coast of Alabama in a small sailboat Les had built himself, and were living on their tiny craft in the Key West Navy Yard and taking their meals at Ernest's house or at the Thompsons's.

Ernest, who was just beginning the safari novel that he would call *Green Hills of Africa,* dropped the book without a second thought and hastily pressed Captain Bra Saunders into service to accompany him by the afternoon F.E.C. train to Miami to claim his new prize. The cruiser was named after one of Ernest's early nicknames for Pauline, and for the Catholic bullfight shrine in Zaragosa, Spain. It was in every way a handsome vessel, and the entire Mob was on hand at the submarine pen docks several days later when Ernest wheeled the sleek *Pilar* into the Key West Navy Yard, where he had obtained permission from the commanding officer to dock it free of charge. The Naval Station held only a token force of men, and dockage in the submarine pen area put *Pilar* only a few blocks up Whitehead Street from her master.

The crowd on the submarine docks let out a series of war whoops that were punctuated only by Captain Bra's "tie up" instructions to Les and Al Dudek in order to protect the yacht's richly polished black wooden sides. Ernest stood at the wheelhouse controls—he did not add the massive flying bridge until some years later—and beamed. The 38-foot cruiser had clean lines and a sharply pointed bow. On a still sea it could do a full sixteen knots. The cabin slept six and the spacious galley was dotted with bright chrome fittings.

A Wheeler Shipyard representative was on board the *Pilar* when she docked in Key West that first time. He accompanied the cruiser from New York to check out the engines. The *Pilar's* engine room sported a 75-horsepower Chrysler and a 40-horsepower Lycoming that had a straight drive for trolling. The Wheeler representative checked out the engines to his and Ernest's satisfaction and departed. Over the span of twenty-six years (in the summer of 1960 the *Pilar* and the Finca Vigia fell into the hands of Fidel Castro's government), the Lycoming engine was the most persistent problem on the vessel.

Once *Pilar* docked in Key West, Ernest and his Mob set out on short fishing excursions. Les, Al Dudek, Pauline, Joe Russell, Charles Thompson, Dos Passos, the Murphys, and Sully Sullivan were among the first to be sported around the island on the cruiser. Grouper, yellowtail, barracuda, jack, and a few small sailfish were among the first prizes heaved over *Pilar's* sides under Ernest's watchful eye. Ernest was no absentee captain either; he scoured the cruiser, familiarizing himself with the readings of all the gauges; he repeatedly checked the engines, and after a short while bragged that he could "hear" the engine running well. He even gave the controls of the vessel over to his brother Les so that he could position himself amidships and see how the craft reacted in the water. Always on the *Pilar* during those early days there was a formidable air of exuberance, of expectation and discovery, but as always the sporting pleasures had to be divided with his writing.

Shortly after he and Pauline returned home, Ernest had begun the book he was telling friends would be "an absolutely true account of a month's hunting in Africa." In Key West now he told his brother Leicester and Charles Thompson that he "longed for Africa." The nine-square-mile island and the whole of commercially-driven America itself seemed crushingly small to Ernest. The account of the safari took the form of a *tranch de vive* novel and recalled some of his fondest memories. The *Pilar* carried with it an imaginative promise of the future. Ernest said he could not remember being happier.

He declared openly that Pauline, Charles Thompson, Philip Percival, he himself, and natives on the safari would be the characters in the book. This marked the only time, save in the instance of naming Key West attorney George Brooks as the lawyer "Bee-Lips" in *To Have and Have Not,* that Ernest actually owned up to the fact that he used entire people as models for his books rather than the scant parts he admitted to. In the book Pauline would be P.O.M. (Poor Old Mama), Charles Thompson bore his previous nickname of "Karl," and Percival would be "Pop," alternately "Jackson Phillips." The natives— M'Cola, Abdullah, Charo, Kamau, Molo (or Droopy), and Garrick—would all be called by their real names, and Ernest was the narrator.

Despite the alibi the *Pilar* afforded, Ernest worked well on the *Green Hills of Africa* manuscript. As spring wore on into the intense and oppressive heat of summer, Dos Passos and his wife Kate left, the Murphys pulled out, and Archibald

MacLeish, lately a *Fortune* magazine editor and a friend of Ernest's since the Paris days, came to claim his wife, but departed disillusioned with Ernest. Although Ernest still found him probably the most "all-round intelligent person" he had ever known, Archie found Hemingway wearing his fame and fortune poorly. To MacLeish, Hemingway had become a literary bully-boy with a swelled head. MacLeish's analysis was no doubt correct, but it was only a surface approximation of what was going on inside Ernest's mind. Ernest was sorting out his African experience, adjusting to a summer that would not be spent in the cool Wyoming mountains but at his writing desk, and quelling his longings to "pick up and damn hell" go back to Africa. All the while he adopted a sedate writer's stance while the *Pilar* waited in the harbor.

But Ernest was not chained to his African muse, and so there were fishing trips. Late in May a Miami priest named Father McGrath came to Key West at Ernest's insistence; on the twenty-third they spent the day on board *Pilar* out in the stream off the Marquesas. Ernest paraded about his cruiser in the stance of a charterboat captain, using his brother Les and Al Dudek as mates. Between the efforts of the three the priest had a tiring but memorable day that was capped off when he snagged what appeared to be a record book sailfish.

Father McGrath fought the wild-jumping sail for almost a quarter of an hour while Ernest expertly maneuvered the *Pilar* into fighting positions. But in the end the middle-aged priest was forced to give up the rod and reel to Ernest, who protested loud and long that there would be no record if the rig changed hands in the middle of the fight. When he finally took charge of the fish, Les Hemingway assumed command of the wheel and did a creditable job while Ernest fought the fish for another thirty minutes before Al Dudek gaffed it and brought it over the side.

The gigantic sail was indeed a record; it measured just over nine feet long and weighed out at 119-1/2 pounds, much over the current Atlantic sailfish record. Ernest—who was secretly resentful that the *Pilar* had been cheated of the record by the priest's lack of stamina—did not let his feelings show. When they docked at Charles Thompson's docks near the icehouse at the foot of Caroline Street, he was raising all manner of "happy hell," Charles Thompson observed.

They iced the big fish down, cleaned the *Pilar*, and then docked her at her berth in the submarine pens to adjourn home to "Toast the good Father," Ernest declared.

All evening Ernest sang Father McGrath's praises, but when the priest returned to Miami, he typed out an anonymous story for the *Herald* that accompanied a photo of a handsome, moustached Hemingway, posed by the giant sailfish strung up on Thompson's dock, tail first. On the front page the *Herald* credited Ernest with bringing in the fish and although he "balked like hell" at first, he accepted the story. After the fish was mounted by the Al Pflueger taxidermy firm, it hung in the lobby of the Miami Rod and Reel Club.

"It's their lie, not mine," he later told Charles Thompson. "Let 'em hang it in their joint."

The fish did indeed hang in the Miami headquarters and for the remainder of Ernest's life the Hemingway record stood good in Atlantic sailfishing competition.

As the summer of 1934 wore on, Ernest plowed deeper into the manuscript, alternating work on the book with short trips out from Key West. But he longed to put the *Pilar* to the test of an extended cruise on the stream between Key West and Cuba.

One of the major problems of putting the *Pilar* in sea order was a crew. While the Depression had offered many candidates on the island, most lacked the essential experience needed to become part of a marlin fighting crew, a situation where know-how and teamwork were of paramount importance. In light of the willing and variously qualified list of applicants Ernest turned down, one crewman he did accept seemed like the most unlikely one of the group. His name was Arnold Samuelson, and he literally turned up at Ernest's front door.

When he arrived in Key West in the summer of 1934, of all the thoughts bouncing through his youthful mind, three had crystallized and were unchangeable: he would meet Ernest Hemingway; Hemingway would teach him to be a writer; he would be a writer. In his opening statement there on the doorstep of the Whitehead Street house he revealed those three facts to Ernest, and possibly this straightforward revelation earned him a place on the *Pilar*'s crew and considerable attention from Ernest himself.

Samuelson, in his twenties when he arrived in Key West, came to Ernest with some of the traditional writer's trappings. He had gone to the University of Minnesota, and already he had been a newspaper man, a rough carpenter, a harvest hand, and a day laborer. He had bummed around the United States twice, and with his own hands he had built a log cabin in North Dakota and lived in it for a year, writing all winter.

His admiration for Ernest was almost childlike. Ernest was his ideal of everything a writer should be, and the Hemingway prose was "tops."

In the path of such admiration, Ernest played his part to the letter. He invited Samuelson into the house, gave him drinks and a tour of the grounds, and touched on his views on writing. When in the course of their talk the young admirer broached the subject of his love of the sea, Ernest astounded him with an offer that he take over as night watchman on board the *Pilar*.

Samuelson was escorted to the *Pilar* that first evening by Ernest and was given sleeping quarters and a small place to write. His duties were presently expanded to include the cleaning of the cruiser, a task that took him about two hours a day. But he still found adequate time to pursue his writing and to play the secondhand violin he carried with him in a battered leather case.

"The case," Ernest told Charles Thompson, "made him look like an underfed gangster."

His violin playing earned Arnold the nickname from Ernest of the "Maestro," but presently that label was shortened to "Mice." Mice was an adequate crewman while the *Pilar* was in port, and although one of his dreams was to go to sea, at sea he was, Ernest lamented, "a bundle of disasters."

"Mice," Ernest once told him, "you certainly are going to be a great writer."

"How can you be sure about that Mr. Hemingway?" the other questioned, eyes elated.

"Because," Ernest replied, "You aren't worth a damn at anything else."

With only an inexperienced crew available—his teen-age brother Les, his brother's youthful friend Al, and Samuelson— Ernest stayed resentfully at his writing desk as June wore on into July. But he had lately begun a correspondence with Carlos Gutiérrez, the Cuban fishing smack captain he met in the Dry Tortugas in 1929. He proposed that the 55-year-old Gutiérrez take over as mate on board *Pilar*, a task he had performed with perfection the previous year on Joe Russell's *Anita*. In July, Gutiérrez notified Ernest of his acceptance, and by mid-July Ernest had all but put the final details on what was to be *Pilar's* first extended run out in the Gulf Stream.

Only one detail remained before Ernest believed he could set out on a run that would do his new prize justice. He adamantly wanted Joe Russell to go on the cruise to man the *Pilar's* wheel. With Sloppy Joe at the controls and Carlos Gutiérrez baiting and gaffing, Ernest felt confident that anything he hooked from the cruiser's fighting chairs he could land. After all, the three of them had fished together as a team and they had met Ernest's demanding specifications.

But Prohibition was finally ended after 14 years, and Joe Russell was out of the rum-running and speakeasy business. Sloppy Joe's Bar (now Captain Tony's Saloon), was a wood frame building with a cavernlike recessed side room and a rickety archway that stuck out almost in the center of the 400 block of Greene Street. The new place at 428 Greene was three times the size of his old "elbow bar" speakeasy at the foot of Front Street, and Ernest found his good friend doing great business. Though the Great Depression was four years along and times in Key West had never been "closer to the bone" as the old time Conchs said, Ernest was genuinely puzzled at the bar's prosperity.

"Times might be hard, Cap," Russell grinned across the crowded bar top to Ernest, "but ol' Mr. Hoover done put a helluva thirst on all the honest folks."

Sheepishly, waving his hands out at his packed house, Joe Russell was obliged to decline the first fishing invitation Ernest had put to him in their six years' acquaintance, leaving the *Pilar's* captain saddled with Carlos Gutiérrez as the only proficient member of his crew. By the middle of July Ernest had determined that he would spend his thirty-fifth birthday (on July 21) at sea on board *Pilar*.

He had been corresponding with officials at the Academy of Natural Sciences in Philadelphia recently on the subject of marlin fishing, and, failing to entice Joe Russell along, he shot off letters of invitation to the Academy's director and its chief ichthyologist. They hurriedly worked up research projects on the marlin that would require field study off Cuba, and wired their acceptance, putting a shaky cap on plans for his first big cruise on board *Pilar*.

But while Key West's "Leading Citizen" (as the Chamber of Commerce was fond of calling Ernest) was preparing for an expensive pleasure and fishing trip to Cuba, the majority of the city's 11,600 citizens were at the end of their financial rope.

On July 2, the Key West City Council and the Monroe County Board of Commissioners met at City Hall on Greene Street and declared a state of local emergency. In an unprecedented and embarrassing step they, in effect, declared local governmental bankruptcy and petitioned Governor Dave Sholtz to accept the city and county charters.

In their petitions the officials, in part, stated:

> Whereas the major portion of the population of the city
> of Key West is unemployed and there is consequent fina-
> ncial distress, property owners are not able to pay state,
> county and municipal taxes and the County of Monroe,
> and the City of Key West are unable to pay their employ-
> ees and other operating expenses, and by reason of lack
> of finances, both the county and the city are unable to
> carry on the functions of government, leaving the popu-
> lation in a dependent and distressed condition ...

The petition also specifically stated that "about half the
population (county and city) is on federal relief rolls."

With the Depression gnawing away at American pocket-
books, poverty was no stranger to any American city or town.
Many were near collapse, but few were in the dire shape of
Key West. After being the richest city per capita in the United
States in the late 1800s, and highly prosperous until the end of
World War I, collective bankruptcy was a difficult reality to
face. But Key West and Monroe County were indeed "busted."

By July 1934, the cigar industry, which had begun on the
island in 1831 and in its heyday had seen twenty-nine factories
that employed 2,100 people produce 64,415,000 hand-rolled
cigars a year for a $1,000,000 local payroll, was gone. Gone
also was the $500,000 payroll at the all but abandoned Key
West Navy Yard. The Mallory Steamship Line had been in Key
West for fifty years, but it too had closed down. The Florida
East Coast sea-freight business, a thriving commercial venture
that had once required three massive seagoing railroad car ferries, was all but defunct, with the major shipping taken over by
the Port of New Orleans. The current high U.S. tariff on
pineapples had cut down drastically on exports that filtered out
of the Port of Key West from plantations along the Keys. The
local fishing industry, hard-hit by the general poverty of the
Depression and the tight capital improvements restrictions it

necessitated, was crippled. The $100,000-a-year commercial sponge industry moved off the Key West flats to the Tampa area after a blight hit sponges in the early 1930s.

In the end, the local officials were forced to admit, there was just nothing left. Their joint petition said that the city was obliged to default on payment of its bond debt and could not pay the salaries of its employees. The City of Key West declared itself "$113,000 in arrears in salaries to employees," and declared itself past due on additional debts of $150,000 for "miscellaneous expenses."

When their meeting finally ended on July 2, the City Council, with Leo H. Warren signing as President of the City Council, William Malone signing as Mayor, J. Lancelot Lester signing as City Attorney, and Sam B. Pinder signing as Acting City Clerk, "resolved that we hereby surrender to the Governor all legal powers conferred upon the officers of the city of Key West by law in order that he may administer the affairs of the City of Key West in such a way as he may deem proper."

After the meeting a member of Mayor Malone's staff contacted Governor Sholtz, who was vacationing in Hendersonville, North Carolina, and after a consultation with his legal staff he agreed to take over the city in a voice that seemed "flabbergasted."

The following day the governor telephoned Julius F. Stone, Jr., the New Deal's Federal Fund agent for Florida, and from his offices in the Exchange Building in Jacksonville, he agreed to take over the administration of the city and county governments. Stone almost immediately named B.M. Duncan, an engineer with the Florida State Road Department, whose trademark was a large briar pipe that he chain-smoked, to head the day-to-day work projects, and both men entrained for Key West only days after their appointments. By bringing Stone into the picture, Governor Sholtz had shrewdly unloaded Key West and Monroe County on Roosevelt's New Deal relief machine. Municipal bankruptcy posed a unique situation for federal officials, but their overall relief program was set up to accommodate it.

Stone and Duncan hastily met with Mayor Malone and other county and city officials and made an initial survey of the situation. They found it grim. Stone found that "80 percent of the city's 11,600 population was on relief and that a 'means of support' for the other 20 percent was dwindling." With regard to the overall picture, Stone concluded that medical care for a large portion of the community had not been available for three years (1931 to 1934), "the residents shoot song birds" for food, and "steal coconuts" from neighbors' yards; "most exist on fish," he said.

Stone and Duncan set up makeshift offices at City Hall and put into the works a Federal Emergency Relief Administration (FERA) program for Key West and Monroe County under the heading of the "Key West Authority," or the KWA, as it became known.

As the men began their work, they considered three major plans to rehabilitate Key West: (1) $2.5 million in direct welfare aid for use in the city and county; (2) $7.5 million in direct welfare aid to relocate the residents of the city and county onto the mainland of Florida and throughout the United States; (3) A self-help program where 3,000 families in Key West pledged $900,000 worth of free hourly work to rehabilitate their own city, with $1 million in federal money spread over an initial eighteen-month period.

Since the citizenry of Monroe County thought the idea of relocation "revolting," and the FERA thought the $2.5 million figure in direct welfare "excessive," the third alternative was decided upon.

Mayor Malone called for volunteers for the $900,000 worth of free labor the city was obliged to pledge, and on the first day after the call went out in the *Key West Citizen,* 1,000 volunteers had signed up. Despite Key West's general mañana attitude, 4,000 residents out of the 11,600 total population signed up for the volunteer work roll. The number was deemed adequate, though, and on July 15, the rehabilitation plan was inaugurated.

"The primary aim of the rehabilitation project," Federal Administrator Stone said, "is to fill Key West with paying guests."

The program was divided into two initial phases. Phase One was a general clean-up, fix-up, paint-up campaign that was to be done by the 4,000 volunteers. Phase One also included FERA medical aid to needy residents. Phase Two was a more involved program that included the installation of a city sewer system, a central water system, and the installation of adequate street lights. Until the 1934 FERA program was begun in Key West, most of the residents used outdoor toilets for sanitary facilities and drank rainwater caught in cisterns. A few residents, Hemingway among them, had indoor toilets that were fed into shallow septic tanks.

The great majority of the estimated $2 million that was spent by the FERA in Key West and Monroe County while the Key West Authority was in effect from July 1934 until August 1936 was spent on the second phase of the program. Phase Two of the FERA's Key West Authority began a sequence of events—including the formal opening of the Overseas Highway (U.S. Highway 1 from the mainland at Florida City to Key West) in 1938 and the completion of the water pipeline from the mainland to Key West in 1942—that would change the face of Key West from a remote island into a truly Americanized city.

By November 15, 1934, prior to the winter tourist season that traditionally began on Thanksgiving and ran until Easter, FERA had spent $274,000 in the county. The state of Florida had contributed $15,000 in gas tax money and had made the city an outright gift of $25,000 for "professional services." A Key West Hospitality League was created with its headquarters at 313 Duval Street and Mrs. William R. Warren as chairman. The Hospitality League was created for the purpose of catering to the "personal" and "homey" needs of the tourist, and like the host of other programs going on around the city, it functioned with the zeal of volunteer firemen.

The first printed appeal the KWA made to tourists appeared that December 1934 as a 67-page booklet entitled "Key West in Transition, A Guide Book for Tourists." A black-and-white map inserted at the end of the booklet, labeled "Bird's eye Map of Key West for Tourists," put the home of "Ernest Hemingway, the famous author" as number eighteen in a listing of forty-eight tourist attractions on the island. The KWA touted the island city as the "Bermuda of America," and the illustrated map weaved a zigzag route along the southernmost city's narrow streets past freshly painted houses, pointing out everything from a Negro church to an aquarium that boasted a 627-pound jewfish. Ernest was listed in relative obscurity between Johnson's Tropical Grove, number seventeen, and the Lighthouse and Aviaries, number nineteen. But the eighteenth spot was "adequate," he would laugh. He did not, he said, even aspire to compete with such highly placed local attractions as the Turtle Kraals, number three, the Ice Factory, number four, or number thirteen, the Sponge Lofts. Or even the decaying old brick pile that made up the long-abandoned Fort Taylor, listed as number sixteen.

In the front of the booklet were three cut-out blanks on which tourists were asked to give "suggestions for the rehabilitation of Key West." The booklet stated in part that the rehabilitation "is an operation involving the expenditure of public funds, accordingly it is subject to review, criticisms, and suggestions of the public." The KWA was sincere in calling for the suggestions and had brightly colored suggestion boxes placed in the lobbies of all the city's hotels.

Administrator Stone was optimistic about the New Deal in general, but he ended his foreword for the booklet on a note of genuine pessimism that he also had expressed privately as the tourist tide came in slackly on the out-of-pocket island city.

"If the season does not justify this long-range program," he said, "it must be admitted that these preparations will have been a waste of money."

Stone left Key West before the booklet was published in December. On September 20 he was named acting FERA field representative for the southeastern United States, the Virgin Islands, and Puerto Rico. C.E. Treadway, chairman of the Florida Planning Board, took over as head of the Key West Authority. B.M. Duncan also left the KWA on December. He resigned to accept a supervisory position planning bridge construction in the Keys that with the aid of a $3.6 million Public Works Administration (PWA) loan in 1936 filled the "water gaps" with bridges on Highway 1 in the Middle and Upper Keys. M.E. Gilfond, who had been director of public roads for the FERA, took his place as supervisor of works.

The first tourist season went off well enough for the KWA officials, but the isolationist Key West Conchs had a hard time accepting all the charity and advice the KWA and its federally appointed officials doled out.

For his part, Ernest viewed all the "Oak Park-like" community activity with great disdain. Three days after the KWA's rehabilitation program went into effect on July 15, he left town on board *Pilar* for his long-awaited fishing trip.

His passengers were Charles M.B. Cadwalader, the director of the Academy of Natural Sciences in Philadelphia, and Dr. Henry Fowler, the Academy's chief ichthyologist. Charles Lund, a mate on the Key West-Havana ferry, went along to catch the ferry in Havana.

Ernest's party set out from Key West Harbor aboard *Pilar* at noon on July 18. Pauline would cross to Cuba the following morning on the car ferry to begin the expedition in Havana. Ernest, now at well over 200 pounds, his moustache carefully clipped on either side of his jowled face, steered *Pilar* from the bridge in white ice-cream trousers and a white shirt, keeping the sun off his face with a long, green, peak-billed visor cap.

In his cabin below, he carried the incomplete manuscript of *Green Hills of Africa* that was then nearly one-third its completed length. During the coming six-week fishing expedition, the book would take a backseat to fishing, but the manuscript would climb to half its final 90,000 words before he returned to Key West in September.

By 6:00 PM that day *Pilar* had crossed the Florida Straits on schedule to within three miles off the Cuban coast; the Morro Castle tower lights were visible in the already fading daylight. But three miles offshore a water pump on the larger of the *Pilar's* engines gave out, and Ernest was forced to weigh a sea anchor while Mice and Charles Lund tried in vain to repair the damage.

Guards at the Morro Castle installation saw the yacht stopped in the distance and, imagining its occupants to be gunrunners at anchor until night, waiting to discharge an illegal cargo of arms, dispatched an armed patrol boat to investigate. In the dim twilight, the two crafts confronted each other at the mouth of the Havana harbor. Ernest, annoyed, shouted to the patrol boat commander that they were fishermen with a broken water pump and had no interest in heated Cuban politics, only in its marlin. The explanation failed to impress, and the armed Cubans prepared to board the *Pilar*.

In desperation, Carlos Gutiérrez left the wheel and quickly made his way out to the patrol boat in the *Pilar's* small dinghy. Midway to the other craft he stood up and shouted.

"El Hemingway! El Hemingway!"

Ernest had, over the years, given the Morro guards tons of marlin. Hearing the name, the patrol boat captain instantly shouted his regrets at not recognizing Ernest and retreated after his offer of aid had been refused.

After the incident, the *Pilar* limped into Havana's San Francisco docks on the trolling engine. The entire crew slept aboard that night, and in the morning when they had cleared customs, Ernest dispatched Carlos to locate a cook and a mechanic to fix the water pump.

Ernest, Cadwalader, Mice, and Dr. Fowler all met Pauline at the ferry docks later that afternoon in the harbor dotted with Cuban fishing schooners, their sails sagging from the rigging in a still hot air with no clouds. The group took an easy stroll along the docks, then had cold Danish beers at a sidewalk cafe across the Prado from the Capitol Building, and then took a taxi back to the *Pilar* where Carlos had secured a sad-faced Cuban named Juan as cook for the expedition.

When the *Pilar's* water pump was repaired by mid-afternoon, Carlos steered the yacht out of San Francisco harbor for some light trolling near the shoreline. But the party had fished less than thirty minutes when Ernest spotted the red target-practice flag flying above the Morro Castle ramparts. The year before, Ernest and Joe Russell had been obliged to steer a rented charterboat through a hail of target gunfire from the castle while Ernest fought a huge marlin. Now Ernest—with nothing on the end of his rod—was not about the risk damaging his *Pilar*. He ordered Carlos to head for open water, and the fishing expedition officially began in a hail of gunfire with bullets splashing in the water behind the *Pilar's* wake.

The following day, Pauline caught the first marlin of the trip, a 44-pounder that she landed under Ernest's watchful guidance and instructions in fourteen minutes. Later that day they passed the fishing village of Cojimar. It would one day be a principal site for Ernest's *The Old Man and the Sea* and the docking place for the *Pilar*. At evening, they anchored at Bacurranao, the cove village where the British first landed when they captured Havana in the 1600s. Ernest, Pauline, Mice, and the two scientists swam ashore in the clear, heavily salted water and climbed the cove's 300-year-old watchtower that afforded a commanding view of the coastline for miles in each direction and sunned themselves. After a few hours they swam back to the *Pilar* and had dinner. Later they sat on high-backed wicker chairs on the *Pilar's* stern drinking scotch and lime juice while they listened to Jimmy Durante's "Hot Potato" on a battery powered phonograph.

The third day out the party saw an enormous school of porpoise that Ernest estimated to be a mile long and four miles wide. Ernest took movies and Mice took still photographs with his Kodak, while Carlos steered the *Pilar* with the porpoise for over an hour as whole smaller schools at times jumped in unison in the almost purple water. After they had watched the porpoise for some time, Ernest took Mice aside and told him not to try and write about what he had seen in a serious way.

"Things like this," Ernest assured him, "are impossible to describe."

The expedition proceeded uneventfully and, at times, the fishing was dull, but six days out Ernest hooked what appeared to be a 300-pound marlin. He played the giant fish hard for almost an hour while the rest of the group looked on with their customary admiration, but as he brought it near the boat, two mako sharks attacked it. Ernest reacted by shooting at the sharks with a rifle held in one hand while holding the beaten marlin at bay with the other hand. In the end, the sharks cut the line, and Ernest cursed all the way back into Havana Harbor. He was still fuming as his party gathered for dinner at the El Pacifico, an eight-story block building across town from their rooms at the Ambos Mundos ("Both Worlds") Hotel. Not even the smell of hashish from the El Pacifico's basement could dull Ernest's anger at losing the marlin to the sharks.

Dinner at El Pacifico was an experience in itself; its restaurant featured four floors below ground and four floors above ground. Hashish was smoked openly in the lowest floor, and the drinks, the food, and the clientele got better as the floors progressed to the top deck, where the scotch and soda set held forth. The restaurant's standing joke was that the smell of hashish was so strong on the ground floor (actually the fifth floor) that more genteel patrons were obliged to hold their noses until they reached the sanctity of the sixth floor. Ernest's party took the majority of their meals at El Pacifico as their routine of fishing the Gulf Stream during the day and returning to Havana at night for their rooms at the Ambos Mundos continued on until early September.

Cadwalader and Dr. Fowler, the two scientists, took notes on marine life, made sketches, and measured the fish they and Ernest caught as part of their research project for the Philadelphia Academy. Ernest's brother Les and Al Dudek sailed over to Havana in Les's homemade sailboat and fished with Ernest. Charles Thompson and his wife Lorine also joined Ernest's party and fished for a few days. When they returned to Key West a friend of Lorine's asked her how she liked fishing, with the "famous Mr. Hemingway."

"Just fine," Lorine said, "but he almost drove me crazy before I caught a fish."

Aboard the *Pilar*, Ernest was judge, jury, and official authority—the "Mahatma," Dos Passos called him—and he would not let any fisherman rest until he had brought at least one marlin over the side of the *Pilar*. Ernest approached fishing as much more than a sport, and he was merciless to what he dubbed "phoney, tourist fishermen."

By then it was mid-September. After almost fifty days on the stream—with the African safari book too long neglected—Ernest and his party rested for a few days at the Ambos Mundos Hotel then made one last run out into the dark blue-green waters for a final day of fishing.

On that last day out, Ernest hooked a colossal marlin. The beast weighed 420 pounds and measured 12 feet in length and two feet across. He fought the monster for an hour and 15 minutes before Carlos finally brought him on board the *Pilar* with a gaff, ending the cruise in fine style.

Afterward, Ernest and Sidney Franklin, the American bullfighter who was then in Havana to promote the sport locally, posed on the San Francisco docks with the giant marlin hung head down and glassy-eyed between them.

They stood on the docks in a slight drizzle, shaking hands around the fish with tight-lipped grins, waiting for Mice to snap a picture. A small crowd of stone-faced Cuban fishermen looked on from the rear. Ernest was barefoot in a tan work shirt and white trousers that were bloodstained and dirty, with a large leather belt cinched around his considerable middle. His hair was combed straight back and receding, his heavy side-burns chopped to military length at the ears, his full moustache trimmed just past the corners of his mouth. All this gave his sun-reddened, face a look of genuine stubbornness. Sidney looked trim and dapper but uncomfortable in a heavy tweed suit and a dark Basque beret and a Scotch plaid tie.

Ernest's party crossed to Key West the next day on a P&O steamship, leaving the *Pilar* behind for engine repairs. Back home after six weeks at sea, Ernest returned to his poolhouse workroom. He immediately set to work again on the African safari manuscript that was two months from a completed first draft.

Ernest completed more than 100 pages of the *Green Hills of Africa* manuscript before he returned to Havana to take charge of his cruiser on September 13. He fished on through the tail-end of the hurricane season, but by October 26, with only minimal luck for marlin out in the Stream, he guided the *Pilar* back to home port. Arnold Samuelson soon departed, his head spinning with all the advice Ernest had given him, and while he did not make his run as a writer [until 1984, when *With Hemingway; a Year in Key West and Cuba* was published], he managed to sell several magazine pieces about his experiences with Hemingway.

The usual winter Mob began to gather again, and when they asked about the Key West Authority's "clean-up, paint-up" campaign, then in full swing, Ernest would bellow "the bloody Rotary at work," and the conversation would usually end at that.

Dos Passos and his wife Kate came down in early November, and the Mob season was officially on again, hampering the much-interrupted Africa book that Ernest declared had been "thoroughly fished on." But the book's first draft finally was finished on November 16.

The completion of *Green Hills of Africa* was celebrated at the new home of Charles Thompson. Only months earlier Charles and Lorine had moved out of the old family home at 1029 Fleming Street and bought an old stone house at 1314 Seminary Street. Ernest liked the house and the privacy its stone fence afforded. He had lately had a cyclone fence installed around his own house, but it galled him that tourists took up a vigil to see the "eighteenth grandest thing in town" walking peacefully around his own yard.

Dos Passos, Charles Thompson, and Ernest had a session of heavy drinking on Charles's porch over a large oak table near the kitchen. The drinking bout was climaxed early the next morning in Sloppy Joe's Bar on Greene Street with Joe Russell stuffing all three in taxis with instructions to "crate the happy bastards home."

Ernest's mood of celebration continued through November; in December he and Pauline and their two sons took leave of the island for a drive to Piggott to celebrate Christmas with the Pfeiffer clan. They arrived in Piggott two days before Christmas. In Piggott he hunted quail but his African dysentery flared up again and he lost a considerable amount of blood. In Piggott that Christmas Ernest also reestablished ties with Toby Bruce. He and Toby hunted; although Toby disapproved of the move he supervised the cutting out of the windshield of Ernest's new Ford. The window was cut out and put on hinges so that it could be let down for Ernest's convenience in quail hunting from the car seat. But as Toby predicted, the hinged window was of little value in quail shooting, and besides, it "leaked like a sieve," he declared. Ernest, still impressed with Charles Thompson's stone wall, also discussed the possibility of Toby's building one for him.

"I'll sure as hell give it a try, Cap," Toby said, and agreed to come to Key West after the first of the year.

Back in Key West in the new year 1935, after stopping off in New Orleans, Ernest had gorged and drunk himself to over 210 pounds. His waist bulged to 38 inches and his size-34 trousers showed "something on the order of a gapped tooth," Charles Thompson observed.

By the second week in January 1935, Ernest—recuperated from dysentery—fished the channels and Gulf Stream around Key West to get in shape for a fishing expedition to the island of Bimini, fifty miles out in the Gulf Stream from Miami. Giant tuna schooled there in late spring, and Ernest boasted that with the *Pilar* he would be ready to take them on.

With *Green Hills of Africa* finished in first draft it was a good winter that afforded much time for fishing and drinking with his cronies. The relaxed atmosphere lasted into the early spring, and Ernest even took in most of the semi-pro city base-ball games that were played on a scruffy crabgrass diamond near the Garrison Bight charterboat anchorage. He got to be a regular, sitting in the rickety wooden bleachers, baked almost sun-black from his daily fishing trips dressed in shorts, sandals, a baggy pullover shirt, and peaked-bill fishing cap pulled low over his forehead. The games were played chiefly on the weekends. They began usually at mid-afternoon, a time that afforded him a few rounds of drinks at Sloppy Joe's Bar and a bull session with Joe Russell or Skinner, Joe Russell's 300-pound black bartender who held Ernest in a state not unlike reverence.

As it happened, one of the chief attractions of the local baseball clubs was a 20-year-old third baseman named Bill Cates, who was also Joe Russell's son-in-law. Bill and Anita Russell had married in Key West the year before; since then he had been tending bar for Josie and picking up pocket money on the weekends with the city league while hoping for a break into the big leagues. He got his break early that spring, but not even Joe Russell himself knew it was coming.

Behind the scenes, Ernest had called "a pal of his in New York" who turned out to be *New York World Telegram* sportswriter Joe Williams. After a Sunday afternoon game, the two presented themselves at Joe Russell's Plum Avenue house, where Bill and Anita were living at the time. Joe Williams, sweating in a business suit, did the talking as they stood on the front porch of Josie's frame house and talked to Bill.

"Son," he said, "how would you like to play for the Brooklyn Dodgers?"

Bill, a lanky six-footer with a full head of curly brown hair, blinked his eyes in disbelief and replied, "And get paid for it?"

"Yes, and get paid for it," Joe answered, as Ernest began to laugh.

Without a moment's hesitation, Bill replied that he was "game," and by March he was in spring training with Casey Stengel's Dodgers. An injury to his right arm sent him home from training camp before the major league season began, but by that fall of 1935, it had healed sufficiently to allow him to hold down the third base job with a minor league ball club in the Florida State League.

During the off-season that year, Bill kept in shape by sparring with Ernest, but they stopped after Ernest drew blood.

"You're my friend," Ernest said simply. "We don't fight any more."

Although Bill Cates did not make the big leagues, he did become a legend around Key West, eventually becoming the city's recreation director. His friendship with Ernest, like that of so many others in Key West, lasted until the end in 1961.

In later years, Bill Cates, not a man to draw pleasure from literature, probably heard more of Ernest's novels talked out than any other person. Behind the bar at Sloppy Joe's he heard the outline and much of the substance of *To Have and Have Not, The Fifth Column,* and *For Whom The Bell Tolls.*

Bolstered by a $5,000 sale of the magazine serialization

rights of *Green Hills of Africa* to *Scribner's Magazine,* Ernest spent his days in dirty shorts and ragged T-shirts, going barefoot to Sloppy Joe's. It was spring and time for the good life in Key West.

Ernest, who still longed for Africa, attacked his Bimini fishing expedition with all the zeal and fanfare of a safari. Dos Passos and his wife Kate were still in town, and Mike Strater, the artist, had lately come down; all were impressed into the fishing party, and all gladly accepted.

On April 7, 1935, a Sunday morning, Ernest, Dos and Kate, and Mike Strater, with a crew consisting of Bread Pinder and another lanky, sun-creased Conch named Hamilton Adams finally set out for Bimini. The island lay some 230 nautical miles northeast of Key West, directly in the path of the Gulf Stream.

What happened to Ernest when they cleared the Key West harbor was almost comical. He hooked a large shark, finally fought him alongside the *Pilar,* and got in position to gaff the shark with his left hand while he held his pistol with his right hand. Once the shark was by the boat, he let go with a volley of shots.

In all the confusion Dos noticed an extreme amount of blood on the deck beneath Ernest's feet—and, Dos noted, the shark had not yet been boated. Ernest had somehow managed to shoot himself in both legs!

The trip to Bimini was finally consummated on the following Sunday with Strater replaced by "good ole Karl"—Charles Thompson. They arrived in tiny Alice Town on North Bimini late Monday afternoon (without incident this time) and the expedition lasted almost four months.

In *Islands in the Stream,* his novel of the Gulf Stream, published by Scribner's a decade after his death, Hemingway reveals his deep feelings for tiny Bimini—feelings that never wavered. The house he describes in the book's opening passages, "built solid as a ship," could easily be the *Pilar* on that first voyage.

> The house was built on the highest part of the narrow tongue of land between the harbor and the open sea. It had lasted through three hurricanes and it was built solid as a ship. It was shaded by tall coconut palms that were bent by the trade wind and on the ocean side you could walk out of the door and down the bluff across the white sand and into the Gulf Stream. The water of the Stream was usually a dark blue when you looked out at it when there was no wind. But when you walked out into it there was just the green light of the water over that floury white sand and you could see the shadow of any big fish a long time before he could ever come in close to the beach.
>
> It was a safe and fine place to bathe in the day but it was no place to swim at night. At night the sharks came in close to the beach, hunting in the edge of the Stream and from the upper porch of the house on quiet nights you could hear the splashing of the fish they hunted and if you went down to the beach you could see the phosphorescent wakes they made in the water. At night the sharks had no fear and everything else feared them. But in the day they stayed out away from the clear white sand and if they did come in you could see their shadows a long way away.
>
> *Islands in the Stream*

The tuna did not make their appearance early that year, and after they arrived Ernest had ample time for his legs to heal before he attacked the fighting fish. His general mood of celebration continued through April.

"We sort of took the place over," Charles Thompson recalled. "Old Ernest was in his glory, that's for sure."

By late April Mike Strater and Ernest began the sometimes boring task of trolling for tuna as Charles Thompson flew home fishless. In the scorching spring sun Dos Passos and his wife spent many hours shell-hunting; Ernest preferred the deck of the *Pilar*. Pauline flew over to Bimini on the Pan American seaplane during the last days of April with the children, leaving Ada Stern in charge of the house and servants. She and Patrick and Gregory, now nicknamed "the Mexican Mouse" and "Gigi," respectively, roamed the pearl-white sand beaches of North Bimini along Porgy Bay with the Dos Passos. "It was grand," she told Lorine Thompson. She stayed for several seeks. In June, Ernest broke from the trip to pay a brief visit to her and the boys in Key West.

He was in Key West long enough to see Toby Bruce arrive after hitchhiking down through Mississippi and Alabama. Ernest wanted a wall built around the Whitehead Street property, and Toby had agreed to attempt its construction.

Back in Key West in August after two months fishing in Bimini, Ernest found Toby Bruce, "going hell among yearlings" trying to complete the wall in the intense summer heat before hurricane season began in September. Toby was making headway but with no small amount of difficulty. A Key West City Commissioner (devoid of any official power as the city was under the KWA) had taken a dislike to the wall that he viewed as "an eyesore," and he used his influence to "bar the Hemingway crowd" from the city's brick sites.

Ernest used a favor of his own, though, and made an arrangement with the commander of the Key West Naval Station, a young lieutenant who permitted him to dock the *Pilar* without pay, to buy some of the city's bricks that were stored on the grounds of the naval facility.

For several weeks after Ernest returned, Toby took a battered old pickup he had borrowed for the project down to the Naval Yard and brought the bricks home 3,000 at a time. As September neared he finally finished the three-sided six-foot wall that ran along Whitehead and Olivia Streets and along the rear of the property. Since it was the only brick wall Toby ever

constructed it was not the epitome of the brickmason's art, but
Ernest was more than pleased with his work.

"Now that I've gone private," Ernest told Toby, "they might
even take me off the tourist list."

Although the KWA did not take him off the tourist list, the
wall did allow Ernest the privacy he desired as he began reading the proofs for *Green Hills of Africa*.

Ernest had not been in the most congenial mood during the
Bimini expedition. Now back in Key West he locked himself
to his writing desk once more. The *Pilar* was dry-docked for
engine repairs and it did Ernest's disposition little good to
observe on the last batch of galleys of his Africa book the
words "is more to follow?" in the hand of the typesetter. He
had ended the book with a five paragraph coda that jumped
from the African bush to the seaport city of Haifa, Palestine.
The setting in the book was a quiet lunch "in the sun against a
stone wall by the sea of Galilee," a month removed from the
African safari.

"Yes, by God," Ernest later told Toby Bruce, "there is more
to follow. But just when and where and why I do not know."

And as was his custom, Ernest also sent off a heated correspondence to Max Perkins concerning the incident. Ernest's
mood mellowed somewhat that late August though when he
delivered Patrick, age seven, to St. Joseph's School on
Simonton Street to begin the first grade. But it soured again
when young Patrick came home with a "D" in mathematics, a
grade that persisted through his first two years at the large
wooden Catholic school.

Soon after he finished the wall during the last days of
August, Toby Bruce left town for Piggott on August 30 with a
friend who worked for the Civilian Conservation Corps
(CCC), the federal agency that supplied labor for the bridge
work on U.S. Highway 1, then in progress. They drove off the
Keys in a light blue Chevrolet, and three days after they left
the worst hurricane to ever hit the Keys struck Upper and

Lower Matecumbe and killed or destroyed almost everything in its path. Hurricane tracking was still in its infancy in 1935, and the residents of Key West and the Keys had only two days to prepare for the storm. The hurricane—they were not named then as they are now—lay off the Bahamas on August 31, and as with all hurricanes the Keys people boarded up and began their vigil. But none of the advance news or warning they received gave even a hint of the devastation to come.

The outer winds and rains of the hurricane passed through Key West on the night of September 1. The damage was minor, confined to light flooding, broken tree limbs, and downed power lines. Throughout the early part of the next day the hurricane lulled in the Atlantic off the Keys and gathered strength, a monstrous strength the Florida Keys had not known in all their recorded history.

That morning, September 2, the barometer dropped past the 29.55 mark in Key West (normal is 30.00). FEC railroad officials dispatched a lengthy passenger train from Miami into the Keys. The train was to evacuate local families, FEC workmen, and the horde of CCC World War I veterans who were working on bridge projects that would eventually link U.S. Highway 1 across the water gaps from Florida City to Key West, thus eliminating the ferryboat system. The FEC train left Miami shortly before 4:30 PM on September 2, and by 6:00 PM it had reached Islamorada, picking up refugees along the way. But the rescue train got no farther than Islamorada. From out of a driving mist of rain at the outer edge of the hurricane that was coming due east along the land from Lower Matecumbe some ten miles away, a 200-mile-an-hour killer wind emerged from a barometer reading of 26.35, the lowest ever recorded in the hemisphere. The wind brought its own killing force and pushed a 17-foot tidal wave across the islands.

From Long Key to Tavernier, in just minutes, there was only devastation. The islands were literally stripped to their bone-hard coral base. The rescue train lay in a swirling mass of steel,

The Key West Harbor and steamship docks at Trumbo Point where the Hemingways arrived in April 1928 on a steamship from Havana—possibly the S.S. *Governor Cobb* shown here in 1934. The tall building in the distance at left, then the Colonial Hotel, later the La Concha Hotel, and the three wireless towers on the naval station were landmarks during Ernest's years in Key West.

The Trevor & Morris Building at 314 Simonton Street was Ernest and Pauline Hemingway's first Key West address in 1928. Their apartment was above the Ford agency where they took delivery of a Model A bought for them by Pauline's uncle.

Hemingway holds a small sawfish shot in the shallow waters of the Marquesas; John Dos Passos looks on. At upper right, Waldo Peirce, Charles Thompson and Burge Saunders show off Peirce's record tarpon caught in the Marquesas in 1928.

Hemingway and his fishing pals rest in the shade of the old docks at Fort Jefferson. In 1936 Waldo Peirce painted the scene which shows, left to right, Hemingway, Dos Passos, Captain Eddie "Bra" Saunders and the artist himself.

Captain Eddie "Bra" Saunders, in middle, was a Conch who took Hemingway fishing before the writer bought his own boat, the *Pilar*. Machine shop owner James B. "Sully" Sullivan, right, was another of the Hemingway "mob." They stand with a huge tarpon on the Thompson Docks at the foot of Margaret Street.

The Overseas Hotel at 917 Fleming Street became headquarters for many of Hemingway's visiting friends. The building was destroyed by fire in 1967.

Pauline Hemingway and John Dos Passos, center, above, stand with a group of friends outside the house that the Hemingways rented in 1931 at the corner of Whitehead and United Streets. That same year the Hemingways purchased 907 Whitehead Street with the help of $8,000 from Pauline's uncle, Gus Pfeiffer.

The Hemingway home below, seen from the Key West Lighthouse. The picture of Ernest on the cover of this book was taken from the porch to the right.

Charles Thompson and Sloppy Joe Russell help Pauline Hemingway display her seven-foot sailfish at a dock in Havana Harbor. Below, Hemingway looks at the huge marlin he caught off Cuba. Arnold Samuelson, an American student hired to guard the *Pilar,* stands beside the fish. Samuelson later wrote of his experiences in the posthumously-published *With Hemingway.*

Charles Thompson with the water buffalo he shot in January 1934 while on safari with the Hemingways. The highly competitive Hemingway reluctantly acknowledged that Thompson was a better shot, although they both had sizeable kills. The rhinoceros below was one of Ernest's many trophies.

On the Serengeti plain in early January 1934, Pauline Hemingway kneels beside a gazelle she killed. Ernest, below, poses with the lion he shot. Later he would recall having mixed feelings about killing such a "wonderful looking animal."

On the Key West docks, Ernest displays two sailfish caught from his yacht *Pilar*. The 38-foot cruiser was built at the Wheeler Shipyard in New York and delivered in May 1934.

Hemingway, at the cabin helm below, described *Pilar* as "a fishing machine." He later added a flying bridge to the cabin roof.

Wearing Hemingway's old boxing gloves, James "Iron Baby" Roberts shows off the fighting stance he used when sparring with "Papa."

The gloves are on display at East Martello Museum.

The Silver Slipper was a dance floor Josie Russell added to the original bar at Sloppy Joe's. In this painting by Waldo Peirce, Al Skinner pours Hemingway a drink back in the bar while sailors and their dates carouse on the dance floor.

Hemingway poses with his family in the backyard of the Whitehead Street home in 1935. Patrick and Gregory stand in front of Ernest, Pauline and John ("Bumby"—his son by Hadley, his first wife).

Hemingway's work room on the second floor of the poolhouse allowed distance from distractions of the family. The large room was sparsely furnished with books and a few trophies of his hunting trips.

"Sloppy Joe" Russell toasts Hemingway's marlin catch. Before Ernest had the *Pilar,* the writer would charter Russell's boat, the *Anita,* for marlin fishing off the Cuban coast.

During good weather in spring, Hemingway averaged catching a marlin a day.

Sloppy Joe's Bar in the late 1930s was on Greene Street where Captain Tony's Saloon is today. In this Waldo Peirce painting, a paddy wagon parks at the corner of Duval. The bar was a favorite of local fishermen and sailors as well as Hemingway's Key West "mob."

Sloppy Joe's moved to its present location on May 5, 1937. Josie Russell moved his bar a half-block down Greene Street to the corner of Duval when his lease expired. Friends carried bar stools and equipment down the street at midnight, and it was business as usual the next day.

Painted by Erik Smith in the 1930s, the scene shows "Sloppy Joe" Russell, Al Skinner, and Hemingway surrounded by their drinking buddies. A copy of the painting still hangs in the bar, but the original is kept at the East Martello Museum.

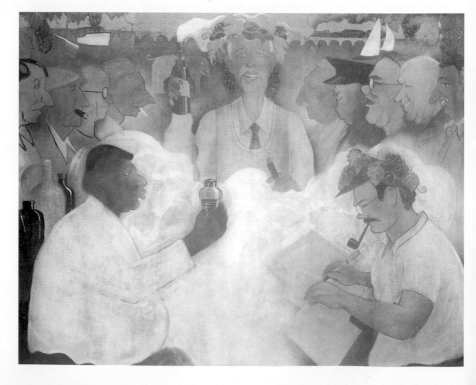

Patrick Hemingway perches on a chair arm between his brother Gregory, right, and T. Otto "Toby" Bruce, left. Bruce was Ernest Hemingway's right-hand-man and took care of both family and property. In 1935 he purchased torn up street bricks and built the wall around the Hemingway House.

Martha Gellhorn was a beautiful blonde and a talented writer. She visited Key West in December 1936 and introduced herself to Hemingway in Sloppy Joe's Bar. After Ernest divorced Pauline in 1940 he married Martha and moved to Cuba.

Hemingway pauses on the spiral stairs to his workroom on the second floor of the poolhouse. In Key West he usually worked from 8 AM until 2 PM producing 300 to 700 words. This would be followed by a nap or swim, and around 3:00 or 3:30 he would head for Sloppy Joe's Bar.

Recently divorced, Pauline Hemingway entertains Key West friends and visitors beside the pool in 1940. Seated left to right are Lorine Thompson, Ester Anderson Chambers, Jane Kendall Mason, Pauline, James B. Sullivan and Virginia Pfeiffer, Pauline's sister. The cat in the foreground may well be an ancestor of today's multitude of "Hemingway cats."

News of Ernest Hemingway's death filled the *Key West Citizen* front page on Monday, July 3, 1961, and local residents mourned his passing.

In 1964 the house at 907 Whitehead Street was opened as a museum by Bernice Dickson. Today the Hemingway House is listed on the National Register of Historic Places and is visited yearly by thousands of his admirers.

its passengers dead, blown out into the Gulf of Mexico, or tangled in the mangrove roots of the islands themselves.

In all, 577 bodies were finally accounted for; most of these were the CCC "Vets." The true number of the dead was never known, though, and the final estimate passed the 1,000 mark by some counts.

Ernest, for his part, with his *Pilar* safe from the storm's wrath, soon toured the disaster area with Captain Bra Saunders and J.B. Sullivan as his crew. He filed a story for *The New Masses* magazine. It showed plainly that the Keys had become ingrained in his system. He had become part of them literally and figuratively. The hurricane disaster made such an impression on him that, although he had become the acknowledged master of controlled prose, for once he completely dropped his literary guard. In his rare and revealing *The New Masses* article (September, 1935), Hemingway gave way to some of his deeply personal feeling for the Keys, feelings that would soon become part of his novel, *To Have and Have Not.*

Human death was not the only fatality of the hurricane; the proud and defiant Florida East Coast Railway's Key West Extension, the approximately 175 miles of track from Miami to Key West, was lost too. When the killer hurricane had passed on September 2, only months away from the extension's 23rd full year in existence (January 21, 1912 to September 2, 1935), the $30 million line was bankrupt. FEC officials later sold the remains of the road for $640,000, choosing the disastrous loss rather than expend an additional $1.5 million to repair a railroad they were forced to admit had never been a paying proposition. The one train marooned in Key West when a full 42 miles of railroad track was washed out by the hurricane was eventually conveyed by barge to Miami, and another locomotive on the tracks was sold for $60,000.

Toby Bruce first learned of the disaster as he reached Evansville, Indiana, where he had stopped to visit his cousin, the editor of the *Evansville Courier.* It was several days before phone connections could be reestablished with Key West, and he waited helplessly for news, after first hearing that Key West had been "blown away."

Toby half-heartedly telephoned Pauline's parents in Piggott to say that he believed Key West had not been hit by what newspapers were already calling "the big blow of '35." The native Conchs, he told the Pfeiffers, claimed that Key West's location with respect to Cuba and the Gulf Stream would always save it from hurricane disaster. His prediction proved true for the moment as Key West was spared, but in the long run the 1935 hurricane spelled a kind of real and lasting disaster for both Hemingway and Key West.

Even before the 1935 hurricane the New Deal was heavily committed to the Keys: local Key West administration as well as the federal CCC and the WPA were present. Now, with the 1935 hurricane disaster, the federal and the state government took an even stronger position in the Keys. They meant to rebuild them; they meant to help the people and they did. But to the hardy Conchs and to artists like Hemingway the changes would be hard to accept.

In less than three years the defunct FEC train tracks would be replaced by the Overseas Highway that permitted automobile travel from the mainland to Key West. Federal housing projects would spring up; a fresh water pipeline would be laid within seven years. To many, island charm was on the wane. Middle-class America was on its way to Key West after more than a hundred years. Although he probably did not consider it then, Ernest Hemingway was able to make his move—out of Key West, in this instance—and did not stay for the full effect of the changes.

5

To Have and Have Not: *Lessons of Key West*

In October Ernest departed Key West reluctantly and, much in the fashion of a hesitant general laying siege to an enemy stronghold, took a hotel room in New York to wait out the early reports on the publication of *Green Hills of Africa.* Privately he considered the Africa book among his best writings, and as a testament of that fact and his friendship for his favorites in both Africa and Key West, he dedicated the book "To Philip, Charles, and Sully." Philip was the African white hunter Philip Percival, Charles was, of course, Charles Thompson, and Sully was J.B. Sullivan, his Key West drinking companion. He had also felt the subject matter, if not the specific content of *Death in the Afternoon,* was "first rate." During mid-October when his novel was greeted with the same mixed reviews that his bullfight book had received he abruptly ended his stay and returned home to Key West fuming, little comforted by the fact that the book was selling well.

Once again the critics had in every sense hit him where he lived. Africa and the Spanish bull rings were his adopted home territory; to reject them as valid considerations for a mainline novelist (generally the most prominent of the criticisms) was to reject not only Hemingway the novelist but Hemingway the man, or at least so Ernest believed. While his short story writing might be going well, he was forced to admit that he had not been enthusiastically received by the critics since *A Farewell to Arms,* a full six years before. And with the literary project that was beginning to take the form of a novel in his mind at that moment, the critic's reactions gave him added cause for alarm.

After having published his first Harry Morgan story, he began a second one. The idea of enlarging and weaving the pieces together as a novel had lately crossed his mind with some frequency. The second Morgan story was mailed off in December to an eager Arnold Gingrich for inclusion in *Esquire,* and later the same month he began a third piece.

The beginning of 1936 found Ernest still in Key West and bitter about the less than triumphant acceptance he had counted on for *Green Hills of Africa.* As usual his Mob descended upon him, so the gloom was dissipated by another rowdy winter season of fishing on *Pilar,* drinking, and banter with Waldo Peirce; Nancy Carroll, the movie actress; Jane Mason; and a host of others who filtered in from January to April when he left for Cuba aboard *Pilar* with Joe Russell.

It was during this time—the third week of February—that Ernest had his now-famous scuffle with poet Wallace Stevens.

Stevens was still an insurance company executive in Hartford, Connecticut. At fifty, twenty years Ernest's senior when Ernest flattened him, he was a tall, somewhat heavy man. Hemingway later said, "…am sure that if I had had a good look at him before it all started would not have felt up to hitting him."

Events began at a cocktail party at a home on Waddell, about nine blocks from Ernest's place on Whitehead Street. Hemingway was not at the party, but Stevens struck up a conversation with Ernest's sister Ursula and did little to hide his negative feelings about Ernest's writing. It was, he told her at first, "not his cup of tea." After Stevens elaborated on literary tea and even further on his dislike of Ernest's writing, "Ura," who at first had remained silent, came to her brother's defense. This egged on Stevens, and he swore that if Ernest was there at that moment he would knock him out with a single punch. He finished his alcohol-fueled tirade by chiding Ursula for her "inadequate" literary judgements. Ura left the party in a huff, returned home near tears, and reported the incident.

Ernest boiled out of his house and drove to the party. To the horror of the guests at the function, he met Stevens coming out of the party, dodged the poet's first swing and, as he later wrote to Sara Murphy, "knocked all of him down several times and gave him a good beating." One of Stevens's punches connected with Hemingway's jaw. It broke not the jaw but the hand. Ernest also told Sara Murphy, "when he hits the ground it is highly spectaculous." The insurance man lay in pain at the Marine Hospital in downtown Key West for several days, taking his nourishment through a straw and keeping his literary opinions to himself.

While Stevens recuperated, Ernest—who always displayed a certain paranoia about matters involving police—went into an exile of his own, explaining to friends with characteristic bluster that he was "in hiding from the law." But a week later Stevens came by the house on Whitehead to apologize to Ursula and to beg Hemingway's discretion in discussing or publicizing the altercation.

In the end, Ernest told but a few folks of the tussle but added, "I hope he doesn't … take up … machine gunnery."

The sale of "The Short Happy Life of Francis Macomber" to *Cosmopolitan* in April for $5,000 took some of the sting out of the limp critical reaction to his Africa book, as its setting also was taken from his recent safari. But Ernest's mood vacillated in and out of rage once more when he arrived in Cuba to find the marlin scarce and his old gaffer and mate, Carlos Gutiérrez, nearly blind and almost deaf.

Ernest fished in Cuba from April throughout most of May while Pauline and Gregory visited the grandparents in Piggott. He returned to Key West during the closing days of May and collected Patrick, who was in the care of Ada Stern, and set out for Miami on board *Pilar* to have the cruiser's larger engine replaced. From Miami, with Patrick, and Carlos as mate, he crossed once more to his "special" island of Bimini. He fished in the "Tongue of the Ocean" off Bimini until mid-July, with *Esquire* publisher Gingrich coming over in June to discuss the third Morgan story. It was Gingrich who probably solidified the idea that all the Morgan stories should become a novel when he urged Ernest to combine them rather than letting them stand as independent short stories.

Five days before his thirty-sixth birthday Ernest turned to Key West, intent on the idea of a novel centering around the Morgan stories, a novel that was to be his one and only book set in America. *To Have and Have Not* did not have a name then and its form was admittedly loose, but Ernest was unmistakably committed to the idea of its scope.

He worked steadily on the idea of the novel throughout the remainder of July, while producing one of his finest short stories, again a story set in Africa, entitled "The Snows of Kilimanjaro." Gingrich readily took the story for a sizable fee and published it in the August issue of *Esquire* as Ernest left Key West's summer heat for the cool mountains of northwest Wyoming and the Nordquist L-Bar-T Ranch.

Accompanied by Pauline and Patrick and Gregory, Ernest spent another splendid fall in the mountains, but his mind was locked in for a good portion of the day on the locale of *To Have and Have Not:* Key West, Cuba, and the Gulf Stream. When he finally returned to Key West in October he was nearing the end of the first full draft of the book. Even with his understandable apprehensions at the critical reception to his last two novels, on his afternoon visits to Sloppy Joe's he was telling Joe Russell and Bill Cates, the baseball playing bartender, that the new book was going to be a "blockbuster."

The return to Key West that fall was delayed by the usual duty visit to Piggott. Ernest arrived in a rather beaten up Ford sedan with his wife and "a back seat full of two rowdy boys." The appearance did not exactly fit the growing Hemingway image, so soon after he arrived he let it be known that the Ford was "going" and that he was looking for a driver.

As it happened Toby Bruce was in town between jobs at the moment, so on a rather cold Sunday morning that October he presented himself at the Pfeiffer house and asked for Ernest. In a few minutes Ernest emerged onto the front porch, barefoot, wearing a weathered pair of Levi's and a red and green and black plaid wool shirt, a two-day stubble of beard framing his substantial moustache. Toby was done up in a pin-striped suit, black shoes, a fancy tie, and a Homberg hat.

Ernest shook hands with his old friend, eyeing his attire.

"Cap," Toby began, "I hear you're looking for a driver."

"I am," Ernest replied, his eyes seemingly glued to the Homburg. Ernest was silent for a moment then he erupted. "Do you always dress like that?"

"Well… no," Toby said, embarrassed.

"Good," Ernest replied, grinning. "You got the job."

They shook hands on a salary of $65 a month, room and board if he wanted it, and "all the booze and cigarettes he could stand."

When they departed Piggott some days later, Toby was at the wheel of the Ford with Ernest in the front seat, a bottle of Teachers Scotch tucked between him and Toby. Pauline and the boys were definitely "second class citizens in the rear," Toby remembered.

When they arrived in Key West, Toby was immediately dispatched to the Mulberg Chevrolet Company on Caroline Street with instructions to buy a new Buick Special convertible, a car

Ernest had secretly fancied for some time. He came back with a dove-gray convertible that pleased Ernest enormously. As a testament to his shrewd business abilities Toby made himself $61 in "kickback" money and had a spotlight (for night raccoon and rabbit shooting) installed on the car as part of the deal. Ernest was delighted. From that point on Toby bought all of Ernest's cars, and became his "driver, secretary, man-Friday, get-away money-holder, and drinking companion"— on salary for the next six years and "for free" thereafter for the rest of Ernest's life.

In Key West late in the fall of 1936, while he put the finishing touches on his "Key West book," a novel that showed for the most part the poverty-stricken plight of the islanders in the middle of the Depression, life had never been better for Ernest himself. After four years of owning his home he had it well staffed with servants, and his life style in the island city was not unlike that of an Elizabethan English squire.

He usually arose just before the 6:00 AM sun; and even in summer his walled-in garden was quiet and cool, and a light breeze filtered in through the open French doors of the second story. With Pauline still asleep he had his toilet in the spacious bathroom off their master bedroom, but he generally waited until just before the evening meal to shave. Still in his pajamas, it was his custom to plod barefoot around the second floor, "working up his juices," he called it, or to check on the progress of the breakfast that Miriam Williams, the cook, who had lately replaced Isabelle, began preparing after she arrived at 7:00 AM. It was not uncommon for Miriam, a lovely light-skinned Bahamian woman of partly Chinese ancestry, to find him sitting at the kitchen table curing a hangover with his favorite medicine: a glass of cold orange juice.

Miriam served him and Pauline breakfast in bed promptly at 7:30 AM each morning; by then Ada Stern was shepherding Patrick and Gregory through their breakfast downstairs. Ernest usually preferred a breakfast of kippered herring on toast and American coffee with cream and sugar, with a small glass of orange juice before the meal. His other favorites included fish roe and on rare occasions the conventional fare of bacon and eggs.

Ernest was usually finished with his breakfast before 8:00 AM. Customarily he would dress in a pullover shirt and shorts and Spanish sandals or moccasins, and then he would walk the short distance from his bedroom across an iron ramp to his second-floor poolhouse study.

In the almost total early morning quiet (Key West then was a more or less Latinized city that did not come alive before 10:00 AM) he would write, sitting in an uncomfortable leather-bottomed wooden cigar maker's chair, hunched forward over a round bamboo table.

He would write on through the morning, and at 1:00 PM Miriam would quietly set a lunch tray outside his workroom door. For lunch he usually had a sandwich and a glass of iced tea laced with fresh lime juice. Bacon, lettuce, and tomato sandwiches were his favorites, and when they were in season he liked fresh tuna salad over lettuce and tomato.

He would break his writing stint after about six hours' work shortly after 2:00 PM. His normal production for the five to six hours' work was 300 to 700 words. When he had completed his writing he would sometimes take a short nap or go to the Navy Yard for a swim (after 1937, when Pauline had their enormous swimming pool constructed in the backyard, he would swim there). Then, between three and three-thirty, he would make his daily trek to Sloppy Joe's Bar.

From the outside, with its rickety front porch suspended by two weathered two-by-sixes, the bar could have been transplanted from a Kansas border town. It was in fact not one of the better bars in the city. Pena's Garden of Roses, The Tropical Club, Baby's Place, Raul's, the Trumbo Club, the Cuban Club, and the bars of the big hotels were done up much nicer and the clientele was of a much more stable variety. Sloppy's was a fisherman's bar that also catered to eccentrics such as Hemingway, lawyer George Brooks, and Hemingway's Mob when they were in residence. It was a rowdy bar with sawdust on the floor and overhead wood-blade fans; a bar where "types" could be observed.

Since its days as a speakeasy Sloppy's had been known as "Hemingway's Bar," an endorsement that meant more to the Chamber of Commerce than to the patrons. It was literally a come-as-you-are, stay-as-long-as-you-want-to bar; open twenty-four hours a day with bands and fist fights and a lot of loud talk. Bar gin was ten cents a shot, blended whiskey was fifteen cents, and beer was a nickel a tall glass. Scotch and soda was the most expensive drink at thirty-five cents, and no matter what you called for you got Teacher's, the cheapest scotch available in Key West. Despite the myth that Ernest drank only rum daiquiris, he seldom had them, preferring the scotch and soda that he got at Joe Russell's special price of a quarter a drink.

On a good day during the winter season Joe Russell took in an average of $1,500 per day, and the Hemingway tab averaged about $25 to $30 per month of that figure. To dispel the myth that Ernest drank himself into oblivion each afternoon at the bar, even with the considerable amount of drinks he bought others or that others bought him he could not have drunk many more than 125 drinks a month or about four a day. There were occasions when the Hemingway tab ran near the $100 mark, and he was poured into a taxi more than once, but these instances were the exception rather than the rule. As Toby Bruce said years later, "Common sense will tell you you don't get dead drunk every evening and wake up at sunrise and write for six hours, even if your name is Hemingway."

After drinks in Sloppy Joe's and conversations with Sully Sullivan, Charles Thompson, Toby Bruce, Bill Cates, Skinner, or Sloppy Joe himself, Ernest would depart in the early dark for his evening meal at home.

He did not take the bicycle but walked down the street. The moon was up now and the trees were dark against it, and he passed the frame houses with their narrow yards, light coming from the shuttered windows; the unpaved alleys, with their double rows of houses; Conch town, where all was starched, well-shuttered, virtue, failure, grits and boiled grunts, undernourishment, prejudice, righteousness, interbreeding and the comforts of religion; the open-doored, lighted Cuban bolito houses, shacks whose only romance was their names; The Red House, Chicha's; the pressed stone church; its steeples sharp, ugly triangles against the moonlight; a filling station and a sandwich place, brightlighted beside a vacant lot where a miniature golf course had been taken out; past the brightly lit main street with the three drug stores, the music store, the five Jew stores, three poolrooms, two barbershops, five beer joints, three ice cream parlors, the five poor and the one good restaurant, two magazine and paper places, four secondhand joints (one of which made keys), a photographer's, an office building with four dentists' offices upstairs, the big dime store, a hotel on the corner with taxis opposite; and across, behind the hotel, to the street that led to jungle town, the big unpainted frame house with lights and the girls in the doorway, the mechanical piano going, and a sailor sitting in the street; and then on back, past the back of the brick courthouse with its clock luminous at half-past ten, past the whitewashed jail building shining in the moonlight, to the embowered entrance of the Lilac Time where motor cars filled the alley.

To Have and Have Not.

Back at the Whitehead Street house, Miriam Williams would have dinner laid out in the large formal dining room. Baked fish and black beans that were always laced with salt pork and onions or garlic were Ernest's favorites. He fancied fresh broccoli with hollandaise sauce, and string beans, and the meals were always accompanied by cold bottles of good French wines. The dress was casual, and usually there were guests. After the meal drinks were usually served on the patio or in the spacious living room. Usually Ernest retired before 10:00 PM, but on the weekends the dinner parties adjourned to the downtown bars and the drinking and dancing sometimes went on past midnight.

Another one of Ernest's favorite pastimes that fall was refereeing the local professional boxing matches that were held each Friday night at a poorly lighted outdoor arena on the corner of Thomas and Petronia Streets. The fighters were for the most part blacks, and Key West boasted a good stable of local fighters.

James "Iron Baby" Roberts was sixteen then and would go on to be a ranking light-heavyweight in the Army during World War II. Kermit Forbes, known as "Battl'n Geech," was twenty-two then and would become a ranking lightweight in the Army. Joe Mills and Alfred Colebrooks, known as "Black Pie," were also excellent fighters among the group. Colebrooks, then fifteen, went on to study music at the Bradley University Conservatory of Music. Victor Laurie, who fought at 160 pounds, and Larry Samber, a black giant, a legend in Key West who always drained a half-pint before each of his fights, rounded out the notables of the group.

All of them at one time or another boxed with Ernest in the backyard ring he set up at 907 Whitehead Street, and all were beaten by him. But as Iron Baby Roberts said later, "We all took it easy on Mr. Ernest." They were, after all, being paid fifty cents a round.

Ernest and Kermit Forbes, a fighter Ernest came to admire greatly, had an abortive first meeting. Ernest—who had let his hair grow rather long in back and had begun raising a full beard that was peppered with premature grey—was refereeing a fight that fall between Joe Mills and Alfred Colebrooks. Through some disagreement Ernest abruptly ended the fight by throwing Colebrooks out of the ring (supposedly Colebrooks had thrown a low blow, or so Ernest believed). Kermit Forbes, who was a close friend of Colebrooks's, went into a rage and leaped into the ring and flung his 5'6" frame on Ernest, hanging on with a death grip on both his ears.

Ernest screamed like a bull, then wrenched Forbes loose, and threw him into the center of the ring where he was pulled out, by several bystanders, still cursing Ernest royally.

"I thought he was just some poor old guy trying to make a few bucks refereeing the fight," Forbes said later. "He looked like a bum with that beard and his dirty shorts. Hemingway, man I didn't have any idea that fellow was Hemingway." When he discovered that he had indeed latched onto the ears of the "famous Mr. Hemingway," he summoned up his courage and—"expecting to get the hell beat out of me"—he went round to Whitehead Street to apologize.

Ernest was very receptive to the apology and admired Forbes's spunk. For the next three years, until he broke with Pauline and moved to Cuba, Ernest became the unofficial head of the boxing stable that included the colorful Roberts, Colebrooks, and Forbes, Laurie, Mills, and Samber. He regularly gave them money and on one occasion took Iron Baby Roberts to Cuba with him on board the *Pilar.*

For his part Toby Bruce easily adapted to life in Key West as driver, secretary, and mechanic in charge of the *Pilar.* Although he "didn't know a damn thing about the sea" at first, he soon also adapted to it. He declined room and board at 907 Whitehead Street or a bed on board *Pilar,* choosing instead a room at 713 Southard Street and meals, like most of the Hemingway Mob, at Mrs. Rhoda Baker's Electric Kitchen on the corner of Fleming and Margaret Streets.

Pauline retained an aloof attitude toward Toby, preferring him in the role of servant rather than friend. The difference between his relationship with Ernest and Pauline was drawn very early when Pauline decided that Toby should wear a khaki outfit when on board *Pilar.* Pauline's accent pronounced the word khaki like "cocky" and Toby clearly won the point by saying to Ernest that he was "cocky" enough "without khakis."

For their main contribution that fall, Patrick, age eight, and Gregory, age five, painted two of the growing hoard of Hemingway cats a dark green. Toby was assigned the task of cleaning them up, but he did not succeed. Ernest retaliated by threatening to paint the boys green; after they saw the grisly end the two cats met, "they hid from Papa for a week," Toby later remembered.

As the fall wore on and 1937 neared, Ernest continued work on the Harry Morgan stories that, for all intent, were now welded together in the form *To Have and Have Not* would assume when published. As usual he fished and drank with his cronies, many of whom were solidly written into the pages of the new novel.

George Brooks was one of Ernest's staunchest drinking companions that fall, and as bartender Bill Cates remembered it, "he left Papa way behind when it came to the sauce."

George had been elected State Attorney for Monroe County shortly after he finished law school in the late 1920s. He had always been a social drinker, but after 1935, when his "girl-friend" was supposedly killed in the Matecumbe hurricane disaster, he "went on the bottle," Bill Cates observed. His office was located at 215 Duval Street, in the building where Shorty's Diner became an island landmark. When he drank in Sloppy Joe's, he had scotch and sodas on a tab for his legal services for Joe Russell. He was ticketed with the name "Bee-lips" because of the curious way he wrapped his lips around the Chesterfields he chain-smoked. And although he stood 5'6" and weighed only 110 with his clothes on, "he was for-ever deviling Papa," Bill Cates recalled.

"He and Papa were the best of friends," Cates said. "But when Georgie would get to drinking his mind just seemed to naturally turn to ways of making life miserable for the old man

(Hemingway)."

George's favorite trick was to latch onto the homosexuals who wandered into Sloppy's in search of sailors. "'Oh hell yes,'" he would regale them, Bill Cates said, "'Hemingway's as queer as a three dollar bill. Just go up to him and give him a big kiss and tell him you love him.'"

The first time it happened Bill Cates said Ernest "stood still and turned as white as a ghost. The guy ran up to him and kissed him and screamed, 'Oh, Mr. Hemingway, I love you.' Papa stood there for a second, spit, and then hit the guy with a right that knocked him out cold. Then Papa turned on Georgie and said, 'I know you're behind this you conniving son-of-a-bitch, I know it.'

'Not me,' George replied. 'The poor bastard was a genuine fan of yours; he told me so.'"

"Time and again George pulled that gag on Papa," Bill Cates said. "Some times I thought the old man looked like he wanted to Kill Georgie."

Another time George and a friend had been sitting in Sloppy Joe's long enough to be about half drunk when Toby Bruce walked in.

"Hemingway's henchman," Brooks taunted when Toby entered the bar. Toby shook his head at the banter and sat down beside the two and ordered a drink. "We're going to get the bastard," George erupted all at once, obviously meaning they were planning to rig something for Ernest.

"How?" Toby questioned.

"Baseball bat," George slurred.

Toby laughed and then thought for a moment. "Won't work," Toby declared. "His head's too hard."

"What do you propose then?" George asked, sinking into a mood of dejection.

"Crowbar," Toby replied without hesitation.

"Hell of an idea," said George, his mood polarizing into delight. "Let's drink to it."

They ordered a new round of drinks but midway through them George fell into despair again.

"What's wrong?" Toby asked.

"The fight's off."

"Why?"

"I can't lift a crowbar," George said.

On still another occasion George Brooks spent an entire afternoon filling a burly Navy chief petty officer full of drinks and "putting him up to fight the old man," Bill Cates said. "Georgie told the chief over and over 'Hemingway hates the Navy; runs it down all the time; never shuts up about it.'"

The chief, filled with drinks and primed like a keg of dynamite, was ready and waiting near the door of Sloppy Joe's for Ernest to arrive shortly after 3:30 PM. Ernest swept into the bar like a charging bull in a bad humor, Bill Cates remembered.

"His clothes were literally covered with dried fish blood. He smelled bad, and he looked like he hadn't shaved for a week. He'd probably just come off of the *Pilar*, and at times like that all he wanted was a drink, not conversation, let alone Georgie's foolishness. Come to think of it," he added, "the old man looked like something out of a horror movie."

The chief was obviously not prepared for the appearance Ernest presented, but George's goading and the afternoon's liquor had pushed him too far. "I'm gonna beat hell out of you for bad-mouthing the U.S. Navy," the chief bellowed at Ernest, but keeping his distance. Ernest took one look at George Brooks and realized that it was all a put-up job. "Bad-mouthing the Navy? Hell!" Ernest explained, pointing to his soiled clothes "I just got through beating hell out of an Army bastard who was bad-mouthing the Navy."

The thoroughly confused chief looked over at George Brooks, who was "laughing like hell," and then he turned to Ernest and said "Mister, I'm gonna buy you a damn drink."

"But Papa was always good-natured about Georgie's foolishness. People in Key West were always rigging people like that in the old days," Bill Cates said.

"One time Papa and I were eating lunch together in the Busy Bee restaurant on Simonton Street and a Cuban by the name of Avilia came in," Bill remembered.

"You give me nickel," he said to Ernest. "You no got nickel, dime be more better."

"What do you want the money for?" Ernest asked.

"Hungry; no eat long time now," Avilia said.

"Papa had the owner bring Avilia anything he wanted. And the little squirt sat there and ate twelve giant hamburgers and drank twelve soft drinks, Papa beaming with admiration all the while," Bill said.

In part Bill Cates was right. Ernest did take all the ribbing in good-natured fashion, but as always he was also cataloging the experiences; in the fall of 1936, they were finding their way into the novel. Key Westers who read it did not need a great deal of detective work to decipher the models for the characters in the novel.

Although Ernest singled out George Brooks and in the presence of Bill Cates told him he "was Bee-Lips," Joe Russell was almost instantly recognizable as "Freddy Wallace," the owner of "Freddy's" bar. The fictional description of Freddy Wallace's charterboat *Queen Conch* was obviously patterned after Joe Russell's *Anita*.

> "Freddy Wallace's boat, the *Queen Conch,* 34 feet long, with a V number out of Tampa, was painted white; the forward deck was painted a color called Frolic green and the inside of the cockpit was painted Frolic green. The top of the house was painted the same color. Her name and home port, Key West, Fla., were painted in black across her stern. She was not equipped with outriggers and had no mast. She was equipped with glass windshields, one of which, that forward of the wheel, was broken."
>
> *To Have and Have Not*

Ernest pinpointed Joe Russell in the novel, though, when he had Freddy install a grating over the hard cement floor of his bar because his legs hurt him. Joe Russell aired this complaint to Ernest repeatedly. And, like Joe Russell, the fictional Harry Morgan was also a charterboatman and rum-runner, a reality that actually gave Russell two parts in the novel, sharing the character of Morgan with Ernest himself who had recently experienced a lame right arm (by a broken bone as opposed to Harry Morgan's being shot).

The stoic and sarcastic Captain Willie Adams, "an old man in a felt hat and a windbreaker," was obviously Captain Eddie "Bra" Saunders.

The price of food was a prime concern for Conchs, most of whom were near a starvation diet then. As a mirror to Captain Bra's own indignation toward the federal Key West Authority and the New Deal machine in Key West, Captain Willie in the novel chided a high government official out for the day on his charterboat: "Ain't you mixed up in the prices of things we eat or something? Ain't that it? Making the grits cost more than the grunts?"

Joe Lowe, a local fisherman killed in the 1935 hurricane, was the pattern for Eddy Marshall, one of Harry Morgan's "rummy" mates, described in the novel as "looking taller and sloppier than ever. He walked with his joints all slung wrong."

James Laughton, who told Professor MacWalsey "I'm a writer," and received the Hemingwaylike sarcasm reserved for nonproductive writers, "Do you write often?" was patterned after Jack Coles, a friend of John Dos Passos. Coles's wife also was rather bitterly satirized as Laughton's wife in a barroom exchange in Freddy's.

Harry Burns, an English professor from the University of Washington whom Ernest had met during the previous summer, served as a model for the "rummy professor," John MacWalsey. MacWalsey, paraphrasing one of the Key West Authority's booklets of the period, said of Key West, "It's a strange place. Fascinating, really. They call it the Gibraltar of America and it's three hundred miles south of Cairo, Egypt."

Albert, who narrates "Albert Speaking" in Part Three, was patterned after Albert "Old Bread" Pinder, and Hamilton "Sack of Ham" Adams.

In a novel in part committed to political comment on the New Deal in general and the Key West Authority and relief program in point, Albert gives Harry Morgan a much less charitable view of the New Deal's efforts in Key West when he tells him that he is "working on the relief."

> "What doing?"
> "Digging the sewer, taking the old street car rails up."
> "What do you get?"
> "Seven and a half."
> "A week?"
> "What do you think?"
>
> *To Have and Have Not*

The wage of $7.50 a week was considered by some hard-bitten Conchs as a greater insult than starving; they had, after all, gained their nickname because their forefathers had in essence said that they could survive on conch meat for the sake of their beliefs. And while most Conchs restrained themselves from biting the federal hand that was feeding them, most were reluctant to shake it.

Probably nowhere in the novel or in the Depression-bogged Key West it mirrored was the *have* and *have not* gap more apparent than in Ernest's portrayal of the down-and-out "vets," the "Bonus Marchers" left over from a war that was no longer a reality. They were no longer the heroic doughboys home from the front; they were bums and a political headache to an administration swallowed up by a snowballing welfare state. After several years of viewing them first-hand in Joe Russell's bar and in and around Key West, Ernest Hemingway set the latter part of their lives down on paper in masterful form, using

Sloppy Joe's as his setting:

> They were opposite the brightly lighted open front of
> Freddy's place and it was jammed to the sidewalk. Men
> in dungarees, some bareheaded, others in caps, old serv-
> ice hats and in cardboard helmets, crowded the bar three
> deep, and the loud-speaking nickel-in-the-slot phono-
> graph was playing "Isle of Capri." As they pulled up a
> man came hurtling out of the open door, another man on
> top of him. They fell and rolled on the sidewalk, and the
> man on top, holding the other's hair in both hands,
> banged his head up and down on the cement, making a
> sickening noise. No one at the bar was paying any atten-
> tion.
>
> *To Have and Have Not*

In a way, the characters in the novel only represented the
struggle of the *have nots* against the *haves*. Using the vets,
Ernest moved from the local phenomenon of the Conchs to the
national "have" and "have-not" gap that the Depression created in America. In one sentence, from an exchange as the sheriff began to arrest one of the two fighting vets, Hemingway
bored right to the heart of the gap:

> "Leave my buddy alone," [one vet] said thickly.
> "What's the matter? Don't you think he can take it?"

Taking it was the plight of have-nots. After more than a decade of taking it, the displaced vets, bunched into CCC camps
all along the Keys and as far as Fort Jefferson in the Dry Tortugas, were perfect models of the effects of poverty and hope-
lessness. Totally physical, with no past, no present, and no
future, they were just *taking it* and waiting for the next drink.

But if it was the vets who personified the polarization of the
affluent and the poor, it was the words of the dying Harry
Morgan that summed up the lesson and the feeling of *To Have
and Have Not.*

> "A man," said Harry Morgan, very slowly. "Ain't got no

hasn't got any can't really isn't any way out." He stopped. There had been no expression on his face at all when he spoke.

After a brief time Harry says plainly the lesson of his life, a statement that might have been the lesson of the Depression, the lesson the New Deal would teach America, the lesson it was teaching it as Harry was dying.

"A man," Harry Morgan said, looking at them both. "One man alone ain't got. No man alone now." He stopped. "No matter how a man alone ain't got no bloody fucking chance."

He shut his eyes. It had taken him a long time to get it out and it had taken him all of his life to learn it.

To Have and Have Not

But in sharp contrast to the insight Ernest gave to the dying Harry Morgan, he himself had a field day with the novel in venting his bitchiness on fellow writers, literary hangers-on, foppish Gulf Stream yachtsmen, and Key West "winter people." But if he vented his anger on others, he also showed objectivity and maturity in including himself in his critiques. If indeed there were sides to be taken, Ernest was clearly on the side of the have-nots. His portraits of them time and again came over as tender and compassionate, while he painted the rich in gaudy colors with searing brush strokes that often resembled lashes.

Hemingway's rich people "with other problems" sat in luxury yachts in the Key West Yacht Basin and worried about being investigated by the Internal Revenue Bureau; they worried about whether or not to take a sleeping pill. Hemingway attacked them as the decadent rich, with their lovers and mistresses, totally insulated from the outside world in their air-conditioned yachts, insulated from the land by their yachts. On the land, the United States was slowly starving on a diet of "grits and grunts."

Ernest himself was very realistic about his own position between the haves and the have-nots. While he plainly saw himself not unlike a seer between the two groups, he was clearly aware that he was indeed a have. Ernest made numerous allusions to himself in general, and his personality traits and habits in particular. And if he was not charitable towards most haves, he was no hypocrite. The lashes he used on them he applied in generous measure to his own back. In the light of events in his personal life before and after the novel was published, the Richard Gordon-Helen Gordon-Helène Bradley triangle in *To Have and Have Not* developed as almost pure autobiography of his relationship to his wife and Martha Gellhorn. It is one of the most personally revealing pieces of Hemingway's writings.

The lessons of Key West were blatantly apparent in the novel—fishing, sights and sounds of Havana and Key West, the peoples of both, the suffering of the Depression and the gap it created (or rather revealed) to America—it is all there. But for Ernest the real lesson of his Key West experience waited for him as he neared the close of a first draft of his Key West novel. The lesson was that the nine-square-mile island was no longer big enough for him; ultimately no single place was big enough for him. Since he was about to be installed for all time as Papa Hemingway, the lesson was all the more meaningful.

6

A Beautiful Blonde in a Black Dress

Martha Gellhorn appeared in Key West in December 1936. Within the four years of Hemingway's writing of *To Have and To Have Not* (January 1933 to February 1937) and its publication on October 15, 1937, she became solidly bound in its pages, along with many of the painful personal problems Ernest and Pauline had experienced in their marriage.

Martha Gellhorn was more than ten years younger than Ernest, the daughter of a Saint Louis physician, and probably the "most ambitious woman" he ever met, Toby Bruce once noted. She had published a novel, *What Mad Pursuit,* and a collection of short stories, *The Trouble I've Seen.* She was determined to be a writer of major stature. Once she saw Ernest on a warm December day in 1936, she was determined to have him too.

Martha had come to Key West on vacation with her mother and brother; while her mother shopped, she set out along the Greene Street bars to find "Sloppy Joe's." Martha approached Skinner, Joe Russell's black bartender, and found out that

Ernest Hemingway did have his afternoon drinks in the bar, on an end stool marked with his name, he added, pointing with his stubby black fingers. Skinner jealously guarded the end stool for Ernest and on occasion even moved patrons off the stool with Joe Russell's sawed-off cue stick. The cue stick appears in *To Have and Have Not*.

Martha left the bar but reappeared later that afternoon and introduced herself to Ernest, who was perched on his stool drinking a fresh batch of "Papa Dobles" Skinner had just made. The Dobles, by then a tourist attraction in Key West, were a mixture of two and a half jiggers of white Ron Bacardi rum, the juice of two fresh limes, the juice of a grapefruit half, capped off with six drops of maraschino, all molded into one in the rusty electric blender near Ernest's end of the bar.

Ernest was almost sun-black from his daily fishing trips. He was barefooted and dressed only in canvas shorts and a T-shirt. Martha had on a one-piece, black dress and high heels; her golden blond hair hung easily to her shoulders, and her shapely legs and long arms were almost snow white. As she took a seat by Ernest, they looked—Skinner later recalled—"like beauty and the beast."

They hit it off instantly and drank on through the mild December afternoon. Ernest, enthralled by the attention he was getting from this blond beauty who was not only lovely but, she said, had read his books, forgot that Charles and Lorine Thompson were coming to the house for dinner that evening. The early dark of winter closed in on the 70-degree breeze outside Sloppy Joe's, and Ernest and Martha still held their positions at the end of the bar, talking amiably while they put away "a run of Dobles."

Charles and Lorine had been at the Whitehead Street house for some time then, and after Ernest failed to appear for the usual 7:30 PM dinner, Pauline fumed.

"Oh, Charles, you know where he is," she said. "Drag him back here and let's eat."

A Beautiful Blonde in a Black Dress

Charles of course knew exactly where Ernest was and he dutifully drove to Sloppy Joe's in his yellow Ford sedan to collect what he imagined would be a "slightly pickled Ernie." Instead, he found Ernest holding court with Martha at the end of the bar in good repair. Seeing Charles, Ernest made a rather shirking introduction and tried to pan Martha off as a "literary fan." Charles saw there was no way to dislodge him and, after he drained a quick drink, retreated to the house where Pauline and Lorine were already seated at the large dinner table.

"He's talking to a beautiful blond in a black dress," he reported succinctly, as he took his seat at the table, seeing no great harm in the state of affairs. "Says he'll meet us later at Pena's."

The four of them were supposed to have gone on to Pena's Garden of Roses on Thomas Street after the dinner, and so in much the same frame of mind as Charles, Pauline simply began to eat the fine crawfish dinner. The news of Ernest sitting in a bar with another woman was not particularly new or disturbing because from time to time he attracted—quite innocently—the attentions of young women who were awed by the "famous Mr. Hemingway." But Pauline had no way of knowing Martha's intentions, and as Ernest sat across town enjoying the company of the "beautiful blond," he too had little idea of what lay ahead for him.

Pauline met Martha later that evening at Pena's. The meeting, as far as Pauline was concerned, was passing and insignificant. But for Martha, who clearly had her sights set on becoming the third Mrs. Hemingway, it was a time to size up the opposition. From the beginning, the competition was unfair. Pauline was small and fragile, with a chopped-off head of slightly graying black hair and a thin face that at times looked hard. Martha, in a word, was beautiful. With Ernest's recent success and growing economic independence with *Green Hills of Africa,* the prospects that he could enjoy the company of not only a beautiful woman, but also a "lady novelist," were imminently plausible. To compound Pauline's problem, as the years rolled by, Ernest's resentment of her money—the money that had given him the freedom to write—had become an open sore between the two. Whether she had timed it or not, Martha, could not have happened along at a better juncture.

Ernest was introduced to Martha's mother the following day, and the chemistry between them worked with almost an uncanny warmth. Mrs. Gellhorn and Martha's brother soon returned to Saint Louis, though, with Martha remaining conspicuously behind in a downtown hotel, probably the Colonial on Duval Street. She soon became "Marty" around the Hemingway Mob and got to be a fixture at the Whitehead Street house. Her pretext for remaining was to escape the hard midwest winter while she worked on a book. If Pauline did not see through the guise, Miriam Williams, the cook, did.

"There would be parties and Mr. Ernest and Miss Martha would be outside kissing and carrying on, and I'd say to Miss Ada, 'Look at that would you.' The way some people act."

The "carrying on" apparently eluded Pauline, or if it did not she did not even confide the fact to Lorine Thompson, and it was January 1937 before "Marty" departed the island city. But even by January it was plain enough to both Charles and Lorine Thompson that Ernest's involvement in Martha had moved from simple flattery to something decidedly more serious. Both of the Thompsons made no secret of their dislike of the budding relationship.

Martha's departure from Key West had far-reaching effects on Ernest's life. Civil war was raging in Spain, and for some time New York columnists had speculated that Ernest would inspect the battlefields and might indeed report on them. Soon after Martha left, Ernest faked a number of badly phrased excuses and took leave of Pauline and the increasingly sedate domestic life that was encroaching on him in Key West. By prearrangement he met Martha in Miami, and they entrained

North together. In retrospect it is not unlikely that he and Martha—a journalist herself—very early discussed the possibility of covering the war together. As Pauline still retained her silence after his departure, it is possible that she saw in Martha the same scene she and Ernest had played out with Hadley in Paris ten years before.

Ernest left Martha, who was en route home to St. Louis, in mid-journey, and continued on alone to New York. There he made arrangements with the North American Newspaper Alliance (NANA) to cover the Spanish Civil War battlefields for $500 per cabled story, and $1,000 for pieces he mailed from the Spanish war fronts. In February, with Sidney Franklin and poet Evan Shipman, he happily sailed for Spain.

The three installed themselves in Madrid in February, and a month later Martha appeared with a contract to cover the war for *Collier's* magazine. Dos Passos appeared on the scene too, and the four of them wandered in and out of the war zone both as a group and alone on their separate assignments.

Ernest, with Martha Gellhorn as his almost constant companion, toured the battlefields for a full month and a half, and he was received by the Loyalists as a man of considerable stature. He early chose the Loyalist cause over General Francisco Franco's Falange. In 1936, he had made contributions to Loyalist medical units and to other groups.

As he walked among the Loyalists, he did indeed take on a commanding air. He was somewhat over his best weight of two hundred pounds now, and his face showed meaty jowls that framed his full moustache. After the lull of domestic life in Key West, Ernest reached out to grasp the vigor and urgency of wartime Spain. He was more than adequate for it, presenting a big, burly, somewhat formal appearance in his tweed coat, heavy wool trousers, and tie, with his large face made even more serious by a pair of steel-rimmed spectacles.

As always in his life, the change that the war in Spain afforded was exactly right for him then. Once more Ernest was moving on an international level, that stance bolstered by a creditable list of publications. Most important, for the moment, his love affair was adding the forcefulness to his life that would enable him to complete his four-year project, *To Have and Have Not*.

On a long-range scale the love affair was forcing him into decisions that would both solidify the accomplishments of his life to date and alter them markedly for the future. But no matter their long-range effects on his life, Martha and the Spanish Civil War were soon put into a secondary position in his life. Back in Key West his home with Pauline and his children waited as well as the unfinished manuscript of *To Have and Have Not*. For the moment neither could be denied, so after a month and a half on or near the front lines, Ernest returned to New York in May and flew to Key West for a reunion with his wife and two sons.

Back in Key West occurred a phenomenon that went almost unnoticed, but affected Ernest for the rest of his life.

"I don't know exactly just how it began but when he got back from the war in Spain we just all started calling him Papa," Bill Cates, remembered. "For one thing," Bill said, "he looked different, older. And his name was in the papers all the time and in magazines. He was always running everything he did. Hell, 'Papa' just seemed to fit him."

Ernest had been calling himself "Papa" for a long while, both timidly and matter-of-factly. After the automobile accident in Montana in 1929, when he broke his right arm, he signed a letter to Charles Thompson with the words "Poor Old Papa." And Pauline had had a foot stool constructed for him shortly after they moved into the Whitehead Street house in 1931, with the initials "P.O.P." representing the words "Poor Old Papa." Pauline herself had been "P.O.M.," "Poor Old Mama," in *Green Hills of Africa*, so a precedent had definitely been set.

But the stalwarts of the Key West Mob—Joe Russell,

Charles Thompson, Sully Sullivan, Earl Adams, and George Brooks—had known Ernest for a full eight years on an equal basis. Over the span of the eight years Ernest had become a novelist of international fame, a big game hunter, a skillful sports fisherman on the Gulf Stream, and much more. Finally, after his involvement in the Spanish Civil War, it was clear to his cronies that he had indeed outdistanced them. And, as happens in any group, a leader was clearly singled out and deference was paid him.

What was built from the affections of his Key West cronies was ultimately the tag, the label for the Papa Myth: the Hemingway Legend. When he returned from Spain that first time, clear-cut labels were pasted on his outsized package.

From the start, but certainly long before the formal pronouncement by its members, Ernest enjoyed playing "Papa" to his mob, but then in the summer of 1937, there was little time for myth-making or legend-building.

In Key West, his domestic problems were swallowing him up, and he hastily put the *Pilar* in sailing order and set out with his family for a summer of fishing in Bimini, putting the finishing touches on his novel, and effecting a truce with Pauline.

The Bimini vacation was only lightly disguised as a reconciliation with Pauline; chiefly there was work to be done on the novel, and he had to prepare a speech for Writer's Congress in New York. Pauline and the children returned to Key West during his absence, but he returned in time to celebrate his thirty-eighth birthday aboard the *Pilar* on July 21. As an afterthought he celebrated the completion of *To Have and Have Not* after four years of off-and-on work, concluding with some of the most concentrated revision he had ever done. Back in Key West, Ernest went about his domestic chores with a sense of duty but with the obvious resolve of a prisoner. By August, after he revealed plans to rejoin the Spanish war effort and Martha Gellhorn, relations with Pauline became strained almost to the breaking point. In an effort to keep peace between Pauline and Ernest, Sidney Franklin came to Key West and packed her and the two boys off to tour Mexico for the autumn bullfight circuit. The Mexican trip was so hastily put together that when she, Sidney and the boys reached Jacksonville on August 24, Pauline was obliged to write Lorine Thompson to ask that her dressing gown be sent air mail to San Antonio, Texas, where they expected to arrive in about a week.

"Jacksonville is hot and stupid," she reported to Lorine on her Windsor Hotel stationery. While the words did not mention Ernest at all, their tone contained about all the kindness and patience she had for him at that time. For his part, Ernest, flew on to New York and made connections on a liner bound for Spain, feeling not unlike a man escaped from prison. In Spain he quickly rejoined Martha and began his trek up and down the fronts.

When *To Have and Have Not* appeared as one of Scribner's fall line of titles on October 15, Ernest was still in Spain with Martha. The reviews again were mixed, but by this time, his skin had thickened. As in the past, the book's sales were good from the start.

Reviewers however, were quick, to seize on the fact that the book was set partly in America, and that in some measure it came to grips with the Great Depression. They saw what was apparently a shift in content if not theme in Hemingway's writing; some referred to it as "transitional" in his development as a writer.

Time Magazine gave the book the biggest publicity in a cover story of October 18. The reviewer relied heavily on the fact of Ernest's current involvement in the Spanish Civil War and stated that the conflict had pushed Ernest into a new social awareness that had given birth to the novel. Of course this was not true, since the book had been begun a full two years before Ernest's involvement in the war effort. But the point was that the New York literary establishment was admitting a new dimension to the "bullying bravo" Hemingway posture, even if it did so grudgingly. "In the eyes of the polite world, Ernest Hemingway has much to answer for," one reviewer said.

Then the reviewer, speaking of *The Sun Also Rises, Men Without Women, A Farewell to Arms, Death in the Afternoon, Winner Take Nothing,* and *Green Hills of Africa* collectively, stated that some critics had thought Hemingway "dated" by 1937, or on his way to being dated even though his collected works had sold over 280,000 copies by then. Prior to 1937 it appeared that "Hemingway was just another case of veteran with arrested development and total recall," the reviewer declared. The review noted that before *To Have and Have Not,* Ernest "Had made himself the principal spokesman of violence, aimlessness, brutality of war and the wartime generation" and concluded that "Violence, aimlessness, brutality were pretty well washed up as literary material."

Although the reviews conceded the acts of death and violence in the new novel, they were clearly impressed by the overriding theme of the book: survival, the theme that the Depression had beaten into America. "Death forms the background of Hemingway's tenth and latest book, his only novel with a U.S. background," a review stated. "But readers of previous love and death stories by Hemingway will find in *To Have and Have Not* a maturity which reflects the more serious turn his personal life has taken in the last year (the Spanish Civil War).

"Author Hemingway can rest well content with the knowledge that in Harry Morgan, hard, ruthless, implacable in his lonely struggle, he has created by far his most thoroughly consistent, deeply understandable character," was the review's deduction.

Except for minor inaccuracies the review held true for the remainder of Hemingway's literary career. What the reviewers did not know, what Ernest had no way of knowing, was that the "serious turn in his personal life" was not in fact the Spanish

Civil War but the increasingly tighter personal triangle between himself, Pauline, and Martha Gellhorn.

Underlying the struggle for Ernest was Pauline's Catholic conscience. And, while she and Ernest were married in a Catholic church in Paris, it had been a marriage under onerous circumstances (the divorce from Hadley), and it had caused her mother a great deal of grief. Disguised as Helen Gordon, wife of Richard Gordon in the novel, Pauline remarks that they have played themselves out. Helen tells Richard, "You wouldn't marry me in the church and it broke my poor mother's heart as you well know. I was so sentimental about you I'd break any one's heart for you. My, I was a damned fool. I broke my own heart, too."

Helen Gordon continued in the novel by focusing on one of the obvious trouble spots in the Hemingways' married life, the production of only two children in eight years of wedlock.

"Love is just another dirty lie," Helen Gordon tells Richard Gordon in the novel. "Love is ergoapiol pills to make me come around because you were afraid to have a baby… Love is my insides all messed up. It's half catheters and half whirling douches. I know about love," she said. "Love always hangs up behind the bathroom door."

Finally Helen Gordon tells her husband, "Love is you making me happy and then going off to sleep with your mouth open while I lie awake all night afraid to say my prayers even because I know I have no right to anymore."

The novel is of course fiction, and in truth Ernest was not quite the "failed Catholic" he boisterously declaimed in public. He went to Mass on occasion and even presented St. Bede's Catholic Church in Key West with a hand-carved altar. Earl Adams, Hemingway's friend since the first spring in Key West in 1928, sums up part of his character succinctly. "He was a poor father and a good Catholic, although he wouldn't own up to either one." But the overall religious strain of their marriage was reflected in the novel.

Helen Gordon, as Pauline, also had some direct thoughts on her husband Richard Gordon, as Ernest.

> "You're as selfish and conceited as a barnyard rooster," she tells him. "Always crowing, 'Look what I've done. Look how I've made you happy. Now run along and cackle.' Well, you don't make me happy and I'm sick of you. I'm through cackling."

Ernest on Ernest in the person of a "sixty-year old grain broker" in the novel was even more brutal on himself. Echoing the words his mother told him as a youngster, he said of himself that he had "an ability to make people like him without ever liking or trusting them in return, while at the same time convincing them warmly and heartily of... friendship; not a disinterested friendship, but a friendship so interested in their success that it automatically makes them accomplices; and an incapacity for either remorse or pity"—which had carried him to where he was now.

> "If you were just a good writer I could stand for all the rest of it maybe," she said. "But I've seen you bitter, jealous, changing your politics to suit the fashion, sucking up to people's faces and talking about them behind their backs. I've seen you until I'm sick of you. Then that dirty rich bitch of a Bradley woman today. Oh, I'm sick of it."

The Bradley woman was, of course, Martha Gellhorn. If Pauline would not make a public pronouncement about Martha, Ernest did it for her. Richard Gordon openly declared in a flashback in the novel that he was having sexual relations with Helène Bradley. Almost as self-punishment Ernest structured the scene in such a fashion that in retrospect it was like finding another man in bed with Pauline, a transposition of guilt and the ultimate marital insult on Pauline. In the flashback Richard Gordon and Helène Bradley are caught in the love act in her bedroom by her husband "Tommy," who was

"standing heavy and bearded in the doorway." And to compound the insult in the flashback, "The bearded man had
closed the door softly. He was smiling."

If the book in retrospect can be viewed as a chopping
block, Ernest assuredly mounted the scaffold with the rest. But
while the affair with Helène Bradley was finished when
Tommy discovered them, the affair between Martha and
Ernest bloomed openly in Spain as the novel rose on the best-
seller list in America.

In Spain for the second time together Ernest and Martha
traveled about the battlefields as nothing less than full-fledged
celebrities, moving as usual among an entourage of international characters, operating chiefly out of rooms at the Hotel
Florida in Madrid. Ernest's writing during this time was confined mainly to the NANA dispatches he filed, but secretly he
had been working on a play since the previous summer. The
reviewers had made him a cautious man, and in the light of his
new writing, caution was well justified. After ten books he had
written a play. As it turned out, the autobiography in *To Have
and Have Not* was only a warm-up for the personal content of
the play that he called *The Fifth Column.*

Late in October he made the news of the play public in a
letter to Pauline, and in November he divulged the play's existence to Max Perkins in New York. Although only parts of
himself and Martha Gellhorn appeared in *To Have and Have
Not,* the leading characters in the play fell just short of bearing
the actual names Ernest and Martha.

Philip Rawlings, the correspondent-counterspy in the play,
was Ernest described accurately from his burly size down to
his penchant for raw onions. The female correspondent in the
play, Dorothy Bridges, was Martha Gellhorn, described from
her blond hair to her passion for homey rooms and the ownership of a silver fox cape. Again, as in *To Have and Have Not,*
Ernest did not spare himself. Speaking to the Moorish girl
Anita in the play, Philip Rawlings labeled his relationship with

Martha: "I'm afraid that's the whole trouble. I want to make an absolutely colossal mistake." With *The Fifth Column* he came as close to autobiography as he would ever venture.

No sooner was the existence of the play revealed than it was shelved. Ernest's role as a war correspondent and his growing domestic problems with Martha and Pauline pressed all else from his mind as the new year approached. He and Martha witnessed the fall of Teruel; by Christmas they were in Barcelona after being on the war front for almost six weeks. Pauline arrived in Paris at the same time, intent on coming to Spain to make a final effort to save the marriage that she finally admitted to Lorine Thompson was "going." Pauline and the boys had returned from Mexico with Sidney Franklin in November, and Gregory had entered the first grade two months late on November 30 at St. Joseph's School, along with Patrick, who entered the third grade. With the children settled in school and once more in the care of Ada Stern, Pauline set out for Spain to win Ernest back. She had gained over ten pounds, her face had filled out, and she was cheerful. She had even let her hair grow long, in a style similar to Martha's, but her appearance in Paris was a "humiliation" that Lorine Thompson bitterly opposed.

Alerted by friends that Pauline was in Paris, Ernest made a shaky pact with Martha to shelve herself for the moment. He entrained from Barcelona to Paris for a strained and noisy reunion with his wife that degenerated into a verbal shouting match which obliged him to quit the war for the second time and sail for Miami and Key West with Pauline during the second week of January 1938. In Miami Ernest sailed the *Pilar* to Key West. Back at 907 Whitehead Street he writhed in the grip of domestic life with children underfoot. While he sulked, Pauline made every effort to keep his attentions from Spain and Martha Gellhorn. She even had an enormous swimming pool constructed in their backyard, then the only one south of Miami. But true to his bullying attitude at the time, he announced to one and all that the pool had cost him his last cent, and to make his point he had a penny stamped into the pool edge.

Home again in Key West, Ernest sat brooding in his pool-house workroom, writing about his recent experiences in Spain and wanting to return. He intensified his drinking at Sloppy Joe's and filled Bill Cates with hours of stories about the war in Spain, accompanied by a verbal run-through of the play *The Fifth Column.*

The best story Bill traded with Ernest that spring was a detailed explanation of how the bar "suddenly got moved." The lease on the old 428 Greene Street location had run out in mid-summer 1937. After Josie had a falling out with the land-lord, Isaac Wolkowsky, he decided to move down the street to the vacant corner building. His big problem was that the fine print in the lease with Wolkowsky stipulated that he could not remove any of the considerable bar appointments he had accu-mulated over the years he had leased the "watering hole." He solved the problem in short order when, at midnight of the humid summer night the lease ran out "every drunk in town just happened by," Bill told Ernest. "They carried the whole damn place down the street where they got set up to a night of free drinks." When Wolkowsky returned from a business trip several days later, he "went into a rage" after he saw the shell of a building that was left at 428 Greene Street, Bill said. "But by then it was too late to do anything."

"Only in Key West," Ernest replied in what was a sort of standard response to the eccentricities of the island, "Only in Key West."

The third and last Sloppy Joe's bar was then established in an arched Cuban-style stucco building on the corner of Duval and Greene Streets, which only recently had been the site of the failed Columbia Cuban Restaurant. The new bar was more than twice the size of the second Sloppy Joe's and boasted the longest bar top in the city.

Toby Bruce was also in Key West then, adopting the pattern of coming and going from Piggott as Ernest went back and forth to Spain. Ernest and Toby fished on board the *Pilar* with Joe Russell, Bill Cates, Charles Thompson, and Sully Sullivan. Sensing Charles Thompson's indignation at his relationship with Martha Gellhorn and his abandoning Pauline and the children for the war in Spain, Ernest tried to justify his actions as if he was only concerned with the war as a writer, conspicuously leaving Martha out of the conversation.

"I don't love war so much," he rationalized to Charles. "War is a bad thing. Death is bad," he said. "But I am a writer. And war is a real thing. I have to see what it's all about. What it is really about," he added.

He did believe he had to return to the war. He was deeply and personally involved in the Loyalist cause, and in the late summer of 1938 when the Loyalists began suffering significant defeats, he again determined to return to Spain and, as surely, to Martha.

So after eight months at home he set off again for Spain during the closing days of March. The break with Pauline was imminent. But for a little while longer she and Ernest could hide behind the pretext of his journalism assignments at the war front for the NANA and the magazine *Ken,* and his work on the collection of short stories and on the play that Scribner's would bring out in the fall.

By then Ernest was a fixture in Spain, and when he rejoined Martha they once again divided their time between journalism and making the rounds of Madrid's cafes with Loyalist cronies and celebrities. After the domestic life in Key West, Ernest was in rare form, back in the air of wartime excitement. But he remained in Europe for only two months; all the while he seemed to be plagued with guilt and doubts about his estrangement from Pauline. He had bounced back and forth from the Spanish war zone for the past two years like a rubber ball. In the late spring of 1938, almost 10 years to the day after he first landed in Key West, he decided to go back one final time to try to mend the break with Pauline.

When he said goodbye to Martha in New York in June after crossing from Europe, they both knew the trip South was in vain. But they also knew Ernest was bound and determined to make it. The visit, more than anything else, was Ernest's living up to his whole lifestyle. He finally realized that each trip to Spain had widened the gap in his marriage, and although he did not know it fully then, the trips to Spain had put a gap between himself and Key West. This last visit was to be a farewell to his wife, children, city, and country.

7

The End of the Best Ten Years of his Life

Pauline's reception was cool, distant, even openly hostile at times. But Ernest was determined to make at least an effort toward reparations for his involvement with Martha over the past two years, and he half-heartedly set out to repair his failing marriage. By then a settlement was simply a matter of indifference to both of them, whether they cared to admit it or not. The sting of knowing that Ernest had been in Spain on three separate occasions with Martha was more than Pauline could accept, and it was all she could manage to be civil to him in front of the children and the servants; their conversations usually ended in heated arguments.

Lorine Thompson's greeting also was distant, and although Ernest soon went around to Charles Thompson's hardware and tackle store expecting a warm welcome from his old friend, he found Charles's attitude toward him restrained if not distant. Ten years had passed since he and Pauline arrived in the city and made friends with the Thompsons; two years had passed since his partial abandonment of Pauline and Key West for

Martha Gellhorn and Loyalist Spain. The Thompsons' feelings had been brought to a crucial point: being basically simple, unworldly, family people, they clearly sided with Pauline and the children.

Sensing Lorine's animosity toward him, Ernest kept his distance, but on at least one occasion he received the full force of her considerable wrath. Ernest was in the midst of firing a babysitter Pauline had used for Patrick and Gregory; Lorine stood by silently until the scene was over and the young woman left the Whitehead Street house in tears. Afterwards Lorine protested mightily, but Ernest, seemingly unmoved, answered her blankly.

"I could see they were starting to care for her too much," he said. "You can love someone only so much," he went on. "Then you have to stop or you get hurt."

Lorine stalked out of the house but later confessed that she felt a real sense of sadness for Ernest, who was himself finding out how much it hurt to love, especially when that love was for two women at the same time.

Ernest soon lost the drive of his reconciliation effort with Pauline, if indeed a sustained drive had existed in the first place. No matter where he turned, he did not get the response he was seeking. Old friends turned a cold shoulder to him while others annoyed him almost as much by "standing on ceremony around him," Bill Cates observed later. Even Key West itself had changed. It was no longer a remote island city. Three months before, in March 1938, work on the last segment of U.S. Highway 1 had been completed. A new kind of tourist now descended on the island: the gawking, nickel and dime sightseer.

If Ernest had not been working on revisions of his play he would likely have fled Key West and returned to Spain and Martha. But Ernest was obliged to revise his play and stories to meet Scribner's publication deadline. As it happened he had only two real interludes from his writing that summer.

On June 22, he flew to New York for the Joe Louis-Max Schmeling fight and made the rounds of his favorite saloons in the city. He returned to Key West with only one thought in mind.

"He blew into the bar [Sloppy Joe's] like a hurricane," Bill Cates remembered later. "Joe was standing behind the bar with me, and Papa let out a bellow, 'Josie, by God, we're going fishing.'

'Anything you say, Cap,' Josie replied. 'When do we leave?'

'How's your boat?' Ernest asked.

'All right,' Joe answered.

'Good. We leave right now,' Ernest said. 'My boat is laid up.'"

During the last days of June Ernest and Joe Russell crossed from Key West to Havana on *Anita,* with Sloppy Joe's teenaged son Joe Russell, Jr.—"Little Joe"—along as observer, learning the charterboat business. In Havana they picked up a Cuban crew of two, a gaffer and a cook, and made their way into the Gulf Stream in search of marlin. For the first time since returning early in June Ernest's luck changed. The fishing was excellent, and the night life in Havana surpassed even that of wartime Madrid.

Fishing the *Anita* off the tiny Cuban seaport village of Cojimar during the first week of July, Ernest hooked what he judged to be about a 450-pound blue marlin. He fought it for well over an hour, the giant fish towing the *Anita* farther out into the Gulf Stream. The small boat was not really adequate to the task of fighting the monster Ernest had hooked, so he used the technique of giving the fish all the line he wanted and was presently obliged to go through the tedious maneuver of changing reels with the big fish still hooked. The changeover was difficult enough for an experienced crew used to working as a team, and when the Cuban gaffer they had hired only days before attempted the feat he cut the line too close to the reel.

With one gigantic surge, the marlin rose and then dived free.

Ernest, in a black rage, leaped out of his fighting chair and pulled the knife away from the Cuban. Then, to the horror and disbelief of Joe Russell and his son, he made for the Cuban who ran for the cabin with Ernest screaming that he would "Kill the sonofabitch," Bill Cates said later after Joe Russell, Sr., had told him the story.

"Little Joe and I grabbed Ernest," Joe Russell told Bill Cates. "I didn't know what was going to happen. The old man had blood in his eye. Little Joe kept saying over and over 'Papa, lets have a drink.' Finally we got him settled down. But the trip was busted," Joe Russell, Sr., said.

Even the fact that they had set a world's record for catching seven marlin in a single day did not pacify Ernest. His angry mood persisted when he and Joe Russell returned to Key West the day after the marlin cutting incident: the mood worsened once he returned home. When Joe Russell delivered him to his front door that afternoon, Ernest could not have walked in on a more awkward scene.

Pauline, who expected him to be fishing off Cuba for another week, was in the final stages of preparation for a costume party she was planning that evening at the Havana Madrid nightclub on Front Street near the docks. Ernest took an instant dislike to the idea and retreated to his poolhouse workroom only to find the key missing. He bulled his way back into his bedroom and retrieved his .38 special police revolver from a bedside table and stormed downstairs to announce that he was going to shoot "the bloody lock off."

Lorine and Charles Thompson had happened by the house only minutes earlier to help Pauline with the last minute party details and they stood in disbelief looking at Ernest with the pistol.

"He was like a crazy man," Lorine remembered. "Waving the pistol around. I didn't know what he was going to do."

Pauline tried to reason with Ernest, but her pleading only

made him angrier. At one point it appeared that she meant to attempt to take the pistol from Ernest, Lorine recalled. "But he balked like a bull," Lorine said. "And then, nobody believed it at first, he shot a hole in the ceiling with his pistol!"

After he fired the shot Ernest ran up the stairs and shot the lock off of the poolhouse workroom and barricaded himself inside, leaving Pauline and the Thompsons stunned in the living room. The three were still sitting in the living room when Ada Stern returned home with the children, who had been for a walk. It was decided that in Ernest's frame of mind the children and Ada should spend the night at the Thompsons' and Charles quickly shuttled them over to his house. By dark, with guests already arriving at the costume party and Ernest still secluded in his workroom, Pauline saw no other choice but to go to the party as planned. They had not been at the party long, though, before Pauline persuaded Charles to go back to the house and check on Ernest.

Charles agreed and timidly approached the steps from the bedroom to the poolhouse only to find Ernest mollified and even apologetic. Ernest even agreed to go to the party, where he made his peace with Pauline, who was costumed as a rather seductive hula dancer. Ernest drank and mixed with the crowd of Pauline's friends, whom he wrote off chiefly as "pimps." He even danced. He and one of his partners, Mary Lou Spottswood, a member of one of the city's leading families, stood talking after a dance when another member of the party approached and asked for the next dance. Mary Lou declined, but the man, who was slightly drunk, persisted. Ernest intervened, but to no avail. Finally the other man took a swing at Ernest, who was pushing him away from the bar. He missed. But Ernest quickly connected and sent the man sprawling on the floor.

"The other guy had had just enough to drink to make him indestructible," Charles Thompson later said.

Before Ernest finally knocked the man cold a total of $187

in damages had been done to the nightclub. Pauline had been "totally humiliated," she told Lorine Thompson, and she went home with the Thompsons that night in a "nervous frenzy," Lorine recalled, leaving Ernest to be poured into bed early the next morning by Bill Cates after an all-night drinking bout at Sloppy Joe's.

Late the following afternoon Ernest appeared at the Thompsons' house; at first Pauline refused to see him. He persisted in his apologies to Lorine and Charles, and finally Pauline agreed to return home with him, the children, and Ada Stern. All four had a peacemaking drink on the Thompsons' wide and shaded veranda near their outside kitchen. Lorine had been cleaning house for several days and had found an inscription on the inside of an upstairs wall. It read "It's a windy day. We want some beer right now." She told the story of the inscription, placed there by Miami plumbers, and drew a hearty laugh, but the strain of Ernest's actions the day before overshadowed them with gloom. "Pauline seemed near tears as they left for home," Lorine recalled. "Ernest was none too happy either," she said.

Ernest's second reprieve that summer came when columnist Quentin Reynolds appeared in Key West. By that time the engines on the *Pilar* had been repaired. Ernest had known Reynolds for some time, and although the columnist wanted greatly to boat a marlin, he knew virtually nothing about the sport. Ernest later retold the events of the fishing trip to Earl Adams in Sloppy Joe's.

"They had been out all day and had had no luck," Earl recalled. "Quentin wanted to land a marlin bad. Ernest was fishing as hard as he could."

Reynolds went below to get a beer and in his absence Ernest reeled in his line and attached a ten-gallon bucket to its end and dropped it over the side.

"Strike, Q!" he called. "Strike, Q!"

Reynolds raced back on deck and strapped himself in the

fighting chair and began the ordeal of bringing the sunken bucket in. Ernest took the controls of the *Pilar* and made the reeling all the more difficult by racing against the bucket. Finally after almost a half an hour of struggling against the bucket Reynolds "smelled trouble," Earl said.

"Look, Hemingway," he called to Ernest, who could bare-ly conceal his amusement, "I thought you said these babies were supposed to jump."

"Oh, hell no, they're full of all kinds of tricks," Ernest assured him. "We'll have to jerk him out," he added, gunning the *Pilar's* engines.

Fifteen minutes later, when the can was finally brought to the surface, Reynolds "exploded," Earl recalled.

"Hemingway, you rotten sonofabitch!" he bellowed.

"You rotten sonofabitch!" Ernest choked with laughter as he retold the story.

The bit of levity with Reynolds was about the only humor that summer. Ernest's mood vacillated in and out of gloom the entire time he remained in Key West. But indecision more than dejection was the keynote of Ernest's behavior that early sum-mer. One day he would scowl at the tourists who usually wait-ed across Whitehead Street to snap photographs of him on his way to Sloppy Joe's. The next day he might cross over and talk with them or hold a sidewalk audience sitting on the curb in front of his gate when he returned from the bar. He seemed tor-mented, and of course the torment was his need to return to Spain, Martha, and the Loyalist cause. Key West itself no longer seemed right for him, friends soberly observed. By the first of August, after almost three months back in Key West, he could take the strains of domestic living and the summer heat of the island no longer. He longed to return to Spain, he told Bill Cates. But his conscience appeared not to let him act. And always there was the final work on the coming book, *The Fifth Column and the First Forty-Nine Stories*. As a compromise, he drove the family to his favorite western retreat, the Nordquist

Ranch in northwestern Wyoming.

But even the ranch had changed. Much in the fashion of Key West, a highway had recently been constructed near it, and a heat wave made the usually mild Wyoming summer little better than that in Key West. Despite all his domestic and logistical problems, however, Hemingway finished the new book in early August. Three days after completing proofs on the book he mailed the preface and dedication to Max Perkins in New York. The dedication resolved his problem and essentially severed the final threads of his relationship with Pauline. The book was dedicated "To Marty and Herbert with Love." "Marty" was, of course, Martha Gellhorn, and "Herbert" was Herbert Matthews, a journalistic acquaintance in Spain. With the dedication as public acknowledgement of his involvement with Martha, the way was paved for a divorce from Pauline. But the divorce from Pauline also meant a divorce from Key West, Wyoming, and his friends in between.

Having finished his proofreading Ernest resolved to return to Spain once more and chose to leave Pauline and the boys at the ranch. During the closing days of August he flew to New York, bound a fourth time for the war front and Martha.

Rather than return to Key West and risk being forced to remain there, Ernest had Toby Bruce come up from Piggott to drive his family back to Piggott and then on to Key West. He arrived before Ernest departed and saw them make the split with a "terrible row" over Ernest's determination to return to Spain and Martha. Ernest sailed for Europe on August 31. *The Fifth Column and the First Forty-Nine Stories* appeared that fall, and as all of Ernest's books had done before, it sold well, placing high on the best seller list but receiving the usual mixed reviews.

In Spain, Ernest once more toured the battlefields with Martha, who by then was calling him "Pig." He was up to about 215 pounds, his hairline was receding, and he gave a stern, formidable appearance tramping about the Loyalist forces' trenches in his heavy tweed coat and his steel-rimmed glasses. He and Martha were now living openly "in sin," he said, and his correspondence with Pauline trickled into silence.

Ernest stayed in Europe until November, but finally, after almost two years of involvement with the Spanish war and the realization that Franco's forces were about to defeat his Loyalists, he pulled out of the war zone for the last time. Martha remained behind in Paris, but before they parted, she and Ernest made plans for her to join him later in Cuba "'as soon,' Ernest said, 'as the Key West mess is cleared up,'" Toby Bruce later related.

Pauline—the center of "the Key West mess"—was in New York with their two sons when Ernest arrived. She had taken an apartment on East 50th Street, sending the boys to a private school nearby. Still pretending that she and Ernest had a chance to save their marriage, she welcomed him at the docks and took him in once more. They lived together in the apartment in a state not unlike a truce until they flew separately to Key West on the first day of December.

The partial dedication of his recent book to "Marty," rumors in the national gossip columns of Ernest's interest in another woman, and the possibility of his second divorce brought Grace Hemingway to Key West that winter. She expected and got a cool reception from Ernest, who put her up at the plush Casa Marina Hotel on the Atlantic side of the island. In their brief talks, Ernest remained noncommittal, and when she left he seized the opportunity to retreat to his old rooms at the Ambos Mundos Hotel in Havana, rejection of Pauline and Key West solidifying in him all the while.

In Cuba he set to work on several short stories about the Spanish Civil War and Cuba itself. One of them that he would expand to novel length he would not finish for a dozen years. He would call it *The Old Man and the Sea*. The story concerned an aged Cuban fisherman who fought a giant marlin alone at sea for four days and was forced to give it up to a band of sharks. It would be his finest work, the critics would say, and it would win the Nobel Prize for him.

He was also, he notified Max Perkins, working on a novel. The novel would be his classic story of the Spanish Civil War. He would call it *For Whom the Bell Tolls.* By early March he was into the book, but its progress was interrupted briefly in late March when he was obliged to fly back to Key West to visit his sixteen-year-old son John, who was in town on a school holiday.

Toby Bruce, Joe Russell, and J.B. Sullivan, Ernest lamented on his arrival in Key West, were all that remained of his Mob that had flourished so heartily only a few years before. But he had to admit he had in fact left them, although Dos Passos, Archie MacLeish, Waldo Peirce, and Bill Smith had by then all gone their separate ways. Charles and Lorine Thompson leaned toward Pauline's side in marital disputes; Joe Russell and Sullivan were engaged in their businesses. Only Toby Bruce was left and in the final analysis no matter what degree their friendship had reached then (and it was considerable) he was in fact in the Hemingway employ.

Ernest's hard-drinking, two-fisted group of artists and writers had been replaced by a more sedate group of winter dilettantes who had gathered around Pauline while Hemingway had been in Spain for the past two years.

"They're not my Mob," he grumbled to Toby Bruce.

Ernest had a good visit with his son John as well as Patrick and Gregory, but "Oh, was that old man tough," Nilo Albury said; Nilo was a schoolmate of Gregory's who often played in the Hemingway yard after school at St. Joseph's. "We'd be standing by the pool," he said later, "and sure as the world the old man would walk along and push us in. He was one hell of a tough guy."

Ernest and Pauline continued a polarization of their feelings, and he spent most of the daylight hours secluded in his poolhouse study working on the steadily growing manuscript of *For Whom the Bell Tolls.*

Again, as in the past, Ernest drew heavily on the people and places of his recent experiences. The novel, set in wartime Spain, almost openly portrayed a number of his Spanish acquaintances, but he also drew again from the people of Key West for the basis of some of his characters.

Maria was patterned directly after Jenny Jennings, the wife of Key West writer John Jennings, who lived in an apartment nearby at 602 Southard Street. Both she and her husband enjoyed a cordial relationship with Ernest. In the novel she is described "in almost every detail," Toby said later.

> "Now she [Maria] looked him full in the face and smiled. Her teeth were white in her brown face and her skin and her eyes were the same golden tawny brown. She had high cheekbones, merry eyes and a straight mouth with full lips. Her hair was the golden brown of a grain field that has been burned dark in the sun but it was cut short all over her head so that it was but little longer than the fur on a beaver pelt... She has a beautiful face, Robert Jordan thought... Her legs slanted long and clean from the open cuffs of the trousers as she sat with her hands across her knees and he could see the shape of her small, up-tilted breasts under the gray shirt."
>
> *For Whom the Bell Tolls*

The tender description of Maria might have been lost in its original form though, if it had not been for Toby Bruce. He was doing touch-up work on the brick fence he had built some years before and when he reported for work at 7:30 AM one morning he noticed "papers scattered all over the backyard." He looked at one of the top windows of Ernest's poolhouse workroom and found it "half-open." Apparently the maid or Ernest himself had forgotten to secure the window the previous night and a strong March wind had blown part of Ernest's previous day's production onto the lawn.

Toby gathered up the pages and, not wishing to disturb Ernest's breakfast, stored them in the downstairs tool shed and bathhouse portion of the poolhouse. But one of the handwritten pages, the one initially describing Maria, caught his eye because he said he "instantly recognized Jenny Jennings." He stuck the Maria page in his shirt pocket and went about his work on the fence. He finished work on the fence, an outside portion on Whitehead Street at about 10:30 or 11:00 AM and went back to his room at the Watross Boarding House at 227 Duval Street to shower and change clothes. When he returned to 907 Whitehead Street for lunch he found Ernest bulling his way about the house "foaming at the mouth."

Toby knew immediately what was wrong and led Ernest to the pile of manuscript in the bathhouse. Ernest scanned it carefully but sputtered, "still... still one damn piece missing."

"The piece on Jenny," Toby smiled.

"Maria, dammit!" Ernest shot back, stone-faced.

"I put that in my pocket," Toby admitted a bit sheepishly, not knowing quite what to expect in Ernest's foul mood of the moment.

"A souvenir?" Ernest demanded. "By god Tobes this ain't the Grand Canyon."

They quickly drove over to the Watross Boarding House and Toby retrieved the missing page of manuscript and took Ernest down the street to Sloppy Joe's for a drink "to calm his nerves and disposition," Toby said later. "He was as hot as a firecracker!"

Deals, old friends who no longer interested him, a marriage that kept falling apart like a piece of mended china, and the increasingly dull night life of Key West depressed Ernest that spring. "And he bucked at it like a bull," Toby Bruce remembered. He refused to fish with old friends such as Tommy Shevlin and Hugo Rutherford, and when "Shipwreck" Kelly, the Kentucky football player-turned-movie producer showed up to talk about a film based on "The Short Happy Life of

Francis Macomber," Ernest was evasive. He and Kelly discussed the proposition in Sloppy Joe's one afternoon that early April with bartender Bill Cates standing across the bartop serving them. Kelly began whispering when he talked of money ($50,000), but Ernest instructed him that, "Anything you want to say to me you can say in front of Bill. I trust him."

But despite all the encroachments on the fruitful work of *For Whom the Bell Tolls,* and Ernest's desire to return to Cuba, some of the dinner parties came off rather well, Toby Bruce remembered.

"At some of those dinners," Toby said, "Papa was in fine form, but he was not Papa." In retrospect, Toby said, "he was Robert Jordan [the protagonist of *For Whom the Bell Tolls*], sure as the world."

"He was trying out his character on all of us. And with a great deal of success, too," Toby added.

By the end of the first week in April, Ernest and Pauline had again gone the limit with each other. Ernest was like a convict scheming to escape from prison. He dispatched Toby to Miami to buy another Buick convertible to replace the Special he had bought two years earlier. Toby purchased a much heavier and considerably better-appointed gunmetal gray Buick Super convertible from Unger Motors. He drove it home to Key West to be delivered to Pauline as a goodwill gesture, and also because Ernest had decided he needed a heavier car for another trip West that he was contemplating.

On April 7, Toby Bruce left for a summer in Piggott. Three days later Ernest, satisfied that the new car would pacify Pauline for the moment, returned to Cuba with a small suitcase packed with the manuscript of his new novel, and took up residence in his usual second story rooms at the Ambos Mundos Hotel in Havana. A week later Martha Gellhorn arrived by ocean liner.

She was clearly in command of Ernest's love life now, and she set out almost immediately to find a house near Havana where they could be alone and where Ernest could work. Ernest was supposed to have located a house by the time her ship docked, but he had not, and when Martha found an old estate on the outskirts of Havana called "La Vigia" (the watch-tower) he went out to view it, but took an immediate dislike to it. Martha protested, but Ernest merely shrugged the whole matter off and took the *Pilar* out fishing. While he was away on the fishing trip, Martha had the old house partially restored and equipped with a staff of servants; when he returned, she prodded him into a second viewing, and at her insistence, they moved in with a lease.

La Vigia sat on a low hill near the village San Francisco de Paula, about a 20-minute automobile ride from Havana. The house and the 21 acres that surrounded it was owned by a Mr. D'Orn, an American with a French wife. Ernest's address at the Ambos Mundos served as a cover that spring and summer while he and Martha shared La Vigia and as work continued on his new book.

He was telling friends that his "juices" had returned to him once more and that the book was going to be his best yet. The novel stood at just under half its final 200,000 words when he and Martha left for Key West in late August. Pauline was in Europe with friends at the time, and the two boys had been moved out of the island city in June when a polio epidemic hit, so there were no "complications" when the couple arrived on the Havana-Key West car ferry.

They stayed in Key West just long enough for Ernest to arrange by phone for Toby Bruce (then in Piggott) to pick up Patrick and Gregory from the Connecticut camp where they had been since the June polio epidemic. Toby cheerfully agreed to accompany the boys by train to the Nordquist L-Bar-T Ranch, and Ernest drove Martha to Saint Louis. Then he went on to the ranch alone to work on the book. He arrived in time to hear the radio news accounts of the Nazi invasion of Poland that signaled the start of World War II.

The climate at the ranch suited him perfectly after the heat of Cuba and Key West, and he wanted to get down at once to serious work on the Spanish war book. But that was not to be. He had been at the ranch less than a week before he received word that Hadley, his first wife, was in nearby Cody, Wyoming. He was obliged to visit her, and the visit came off pleasantly enough with Ernest shaking hands with her husband, of whom he heartily approved. But he had no sooner returned from Cody when Pauline telephoned to say that she had just returned from Europe and was coming to the ranch to be with him when Toby and the boys arrived. She was determined, she said, to make one last effort to hold their marriage together.

Pauline flew in with a severe cold and went to bed immediately, the hope of any reconciliation dead from the start. Toby arrived with the boys several days later, and he and Ernest cooked and kept house while attending to Pauline and the boys. "Pauline was despondent," Toby recalled. Ernest was glum and sullen and did little work on his novel. The moment Pauline had recovered sufficiently from her cold, Ernest asked Toby to get her and the boys back to Key West in time for the opening of school only days away. Ernest then cleared out of the Nordquist ranch and any serious contact with Pauline for the last time.

Although their divorce was more than a year away, when Ernest left Nordquist Ranch, Pauline changed places with Martha as "the other woman." His life with Pauline was "through," he told Toby, and he telephoned Martha Gellhorn to meet him in a small resort town in mountainous south central Idaho named Sun Valley.

In 1939, Sun Valley was a grand but infant ski resort set high in Idaho's craggy Sawtooth Mountains. Ernest arrived there in his new Buick convertible, wearing faded Levi's cinched up with a wide cowboy belt that sported a large silver buckle, and a leather vest over a plaid sports shirt. He was just over 200 pounds, his hair was slightly longer than usual, and his moustache was full and bushy. The knot from the Paris skylight accident still showed plainly above his left eye after more than ten years, and in general he had the appearance of a rough cowhand who had come into town to whoop it up for the weekend. When Martha arrived a few days later, she and Ernest took up residence in one of the most expensive suites in the "Glamour House," the resort's main lodge, at $38 a day. Ernest immediately began dividing his time between work on the novel in the mornings and introducing her to the field sports of fishing and hunting in the nearby countryside in the afternoon.

Just as he had adopted Key West ten years earlier, Ernest now decided on Sun Valley as a home for part of the year. His new Sun Valley friends, who in turn became known as the "Sun Valley Mob," were the resort's chief photographer Lloyd "Pappy" Arnold; an old mountain hunter named Bill Hamilton; Taylor Williams, the chief hunting guide known as "Beartracks," or "the Colonel;" Arnold's wife, Tillie; another guide, Gene Van Guilder; and Spike Spackman, an ex-Hollywood stunt man who managed the lodge's horses. In their own different ways the members of the Sun Valley Mob and Sun Valley itself held that mysterious quality that was totally right for Ernest at that moment. With his uncanny perception Ernest reached out to them. What was even more right for Ernest at that time was that he had come to the resort a full-fledged celebrity. There was no gestation period, no transition from "Ernie" to "Papa" as there had been in Key West and Wyoming. Now he was Papa.

Soon after they arrived in Sun Valley, Martha got a magazine assignment to cover the German offensive in Finland. Ernest said little to discourage the trip, because he was deeply involved then in work on *For Whom the Bell Tolls,* having completed over half the manuscript by November. Martha left during the early days of November. But within one month, the

Christmas season and his nagging conscience, coupled with frustration and hard work on the novel and the Idaho winter, got the best of Ernest. He did a complete about-face and wrote Pauline telling her that an "attack of loneliness" had set in on him and he wanted to come down for the holidays with her and the two boys. Pauline answered that she flatly refused to see him if he intended to continue the affair with Martha. Ernest was noncommittal on that point but persisted in his efforts to have her take him in for Christmas "just for the boys' sake," he said. In the end, she held to her refusal and flew with the two children to New York for the holidays.

Ernest, however, believed she would change her mind, and he called Toby Bruce from Piggott to Sun Valley to drive him to Key West for Christmas. Toby arrived during the second week of December; after a farewell party at the Sun Valley Lodge, he loaded "a much hungover Papa" into the Buick at mid-afternoon December 10 for the drive back to Key West.

The going-away party, thrown by Taylor Williams and Lloyd Arnold, was "a royal drunk," Toby Bruce recalled. Two days later when they left, one of the wives packed Ernest and Toby what looked like "a feast" inside a huge wicker basket.

"But it was only one small duck," Toby said. "Papa got a big kick out of that. He ate the duck, and then said 'Let's stop somewhere and get the rest of the meal,'" Toby recalled.

On the ride home Ernest related the gist of his telephone conversation with Pauline, but told Toby he fully expected to find her and the boys at home. Toby kept silent at the time but said later that it would have taken "a major miracle" for her to have been there. Their marriage was over, whether Ernest realized it or not. All that waited was a formal divorce, although Ernest presumably had not considered that either. Apparently he believed that Pauline would continue to sit idly by and let him choose between her and Martha. She would not.

They arrived in Key West on December 17, and, as Toby expected, they found the house empty except for Jimmy Smith, the gardener, and his three children, who had as usual taken up temporary quarters in the poolhouse. Pauline had given the rest of the servants a Christmas holiday with pay to further spite Ernest, who was obliged to have his meals at downtown restaurants. Toby almost immediately returned to Piggott for the holidays, and Ernest remained in the city for nine days, seeing almost no one, writing in both morning and afternoon sessions on *For Whom the Bell Tolls*. On the day after Christmas, almost as if he had remained in the empty house on Christmas Day as penance, Ernest packed a number of his personal items, books, and clothes in the Buick and loaded it onto the Key West-to-Havana car ferry. He quietly left the island city that had been his home for over a decade. He would come back to 907 Whitehead Street again; he would come back to Key West, but it would no longer be his home. All pretext of retaining ties with either, as well as with Pauline, were swept away on the ferry ride to Cuba on December 26, 1939. After that date his address would be 90 miles across the Gulf Stream on a farm in the sleepy, impoverished village of San Francisco de Paula, Pinar del Rio province, a farm he would soon buy and rename Finca Vigia—"Lookout Farm."

As the year 1940 came in, Ernest was installed at La Vigia; when Martha returned from what he termed "the tax-free wars," she found him working well on *For Whom the Bell Tolls*. He was once more into his habitual pattern of writing in the mornings and drinking and fishing in the afternoons and evenings. He had been a visitor to Cuba for as many years as he had been in Key West; he was an astute student of its cosmopolitan, Latin ways. When Martha returned she found him in "extremely good spirits," well-adjusted, and satisfied to his only slightly changed lifestyle, Toby Bruce remembered. He worked off his heavy drinking bouts by playing tennis with Martha or a group of Basques who were living in exile in Cuba. He had a small stable of his own fighting roosters; he shot white-crowned pigeons for high stakes at the Club de

Cazadores; and he hunted quail in the rugged hills around his farm. As he had in the past, he held court over evenings of hard drinking at the bar in the Ambos Mundos Hotel or at La Floridita. As always, the fishing cruiser *Pilar* was docked in the nearby harbor of Cojimar, and the new Buick convertible was parked at his doorstep.

His finances, though, were not in good order. Less than a month after his break with Pauline he was obliged to ask Max Perkins for a $1,000 advance on the new novel. Most embarrassing of all, he was forced to hold Pauline to a promise she had made him in November 1939. She would help him pay his taxes in February of 1940, she had told him. Pauline told Lorine Thompson about helping Ernest with his taxes, and she went into a rage.

"I told her she was crazy after the way Ernest had treated her. But she said she was going to help him just the same. 'A promise was a promise,' she said," Lorine related later. Whatever Pauline's rationale, Ernest for his part was forced to see very early and blatantly just what the security of Pauline's money had meant to him over the past ten years.

But with Martha caring for him and seeing to the running of the La Vigia household, Ernest worked well on the novel all through the winter and spring months of that new year. By early summer he was approaching the final chapters.

The break with Pauline was final now, and she had begun divorce proceedings in Miami, chiefly to stave off further notoriety and embarrassment in Key West. Thoughts of Pauline, their decade of married life, their children, and of breaks with old friends over the matter continued to nag Ernest on into July, but he made steady progress with *For Whom the Bell Tolls* all the while. On July 13, eight days before his forty-first birthday, he finished the big novel he had worked on for almost a year and a half.

Toby Bruce, who had been with Ernest and Martha at La Vigia for some time then, doing repair work on the house and serving as a private secretary to Ernest, supervised the typing of the handwritten manuscript of the novel in Havana. Once the book was typed, Ernest went to New York alone to present it to Scribner's. He took rooms in his usual residence at the Hotel Barclay, did revisions on the typescript, then returned to Cuba to await the galley proofs of the book.

During the last week in August he mailed the first batch of galleys back to Max Perkins in New York. Then, prompted by an offer from the Sun Valley resort management to accept a dollar-per-day "celebrity rate" for himself and his entourage at the resort, he abandoned the stifling heat of the Cuban summer for the cool mountain air of Idaho.

Martha flew on ahead to Sun Valley, stopping in Saint Louis to see her mother. Pauline, Patrick, and Gregory were in San Francisco visiting Pauline's sister Virginia. The boys were taken out of school there and put on a train for Sun Valley. Ernest and Toby Bruce crossed from Havana to Key West on the car ferry and left for Idaho on September 1. On Labor Day the final divorce hearing was held in Miami, but as it turned out, it was Charles and Lorine Thompson who bore the brunt of Ernest and Pauline's divorce troubles when they stood in absentia for the couple before a Miami circuit court judge.

Circuit Court Judge Arthur "Kitty" Gomez, a former Key Wester and long-time friend of the Thompsons, held the final divorce hearing in Miami on Labor Day, 1940, at the request of Pauline's Key West lawyer, Henry Taylor. Judge Gomez went into the proceedings in his chambers without knowing it was the Hemingways who were getting a divorce, just that a Key West party had asked for the protection of having the hearing on a holiday in order to avoid publicity. When the Thompsons walked into his chambers, the judge stiffened noticeably and fell almost mute before his two old friends, whom he considered "as happy a couple who ever married."

Charles and Lorine quickly signed the divorce documents showing that the Hemingways were residents of Key West, and the state of Florida. But Judge Gomez's reaction had been so strained that he practically bolted from the room even as he read that it was in fact Pauline Hemingway who was divorcing her husband, Ernest Miller Hemingway. Back in Key West about a week later, the Thompsons ran into the judge at a nightclub and they all had a good laugh over the "Thompson divorce." But to Lorine Thompson there was no humor in the Hemingway divorce; as Pauline's closest friend, she knew that Pauline retained a deep hurt over the separation although she continually denied that fact and even concealed it in her letters to Lorine.

Just prior to the divorce Pauline wrote Lorine from San Francisco: "So I am alone at last and having a wonderful time. Will probably stay through this month [September], and hope to get divorced before I leave, but it's a slow business even though the settlement is about drawn up. It will be fine to be a free woman. How do you suppose it will feel?" she said. Lorine, as always, had her own strong opinions as to how it would "feel." She was convinced Ernest had hurt Pauline enormously, and she did little to hide her bitterness at that fact.

Pauline's divorce from Ernest held him to no provisions for child support for Patrick and Gregory. She explained that she did not want to be a block in the way of his writing and would leave what support he gave them up to his conscience. Ernest, for his part, always tried to help the boys, but over the years, his fluctuating financial situation would often not allow him to be as generous as he would have liked. In simple dollars and cents Pauline's inheritance and annuity income were more than adequate for her and the children for the rest of their lives, and she and Ernest both knew it.

In Sun Valley, where his eldest son John presently appeared, Ernest and Martha again were provided with plush $38-a-day rooms—Suite 33 in the main lodge or "Glamour House." Toby Bruce and the boys were given two fine $14-per-day rooms in the resort's inn for the dollar-per-day celebrity rate. The newly formed Sun Valley Mob—Taylor Williams, Lloyd Arnold, and Lloyd's wife Tillie—were on hand to greet the Hemingway party. But reworking the final batch of galleys still remained before any serious vacation could begin.

Working as much as eighteen-hour work days or "table time," as he sometimes called it, Ernest finished the galleys within two weeks of arriving at the resort. Toby Bruce sent off the galleys via REA in three separate batches then summoned the resort's photographer, Lloyd Arnold, to take a dust jacket photo for the book. The craggy-faced Arnold appeared in Ernest's room and Ernest sat at his Royal portable typewriter before a blond desk stacked high with books and papers. His hands were on the portable's keys, the sleeves of his white dress shirt were carelessly rolled up, and a shotgun stood in the corner to his rear by a chair piled high with packages of man-uscript. Since the book was finished, he had finally cut his hair, but "ducktails" were sticking out in the back, curled up like horns. His moustache was full but trimmed, and his sideburns had been whacked off in a short military fashion. Toby combed the unruly hairs down once for the photograph, but before he could retreat from the camera's view they sprung out again.

"What about it, Tobes," Ernest asked when he was told, "should we leave 'um?"

"Leave 'um, Papa," Toby reassured him. "They look just fine," he added, as Arnold snapped the shutter of his camera.

Toby Bruce had been instrumental in helping Ernest through both his difficult personal problems and even the liter-ary problems of writing *For Whom the Bell Tolls.* He was there as a buffer between Pauline and Martha—a link between the past and future—and he read every word of the novel as it was being written. He had handled Ernest's voluminous correspon-dence for the past year and a half. "The Iron Man," Ernest now called him, and for his contribution on the project he gave him the commission to design the novel's dust jacket. Toby decided on a scenic drawing that was both realistic and a composite of themes and ideas from the novel. Toby's rough sketch showed a tiny village nestled at the foot of a small mountain, a bell tower, and the woods with the outline of the bridge blown up by Robert Jordan in the novel. An artist in New York did the actual finished drawing, but Ernest proudly told one and all that it was "the Iron Man's masterpiece."

Ernest also presented Toby with the final galleys of the novel, showing most of his penciled corrections, a handsome leather-bound edition inscribed "To Otto [Toby's middle name] with much affection and deep appreciation for all he did to make this book. Ernest Hemingway." When he gave Toby the galleys he told him that it was his "insurance policy. Its value will go up with Hemingstein stock," he told his friend; "Let's hope the company doesn't run dry!"

The novel that appeared at the top of Scribner's line that fall did indeed raise the "Hemingstein stock." It made Ernest rich. The Book of the Month Club made the novel their October selection and ordered 200,000 copies. Scribner's published a regular trade edition of 160,000 copies; the movie rights were sold for $100,000, at that time the highest price ever paid for film rights to to a novel. Moreover, from a literary standpoint, the novel was received by the critics as the work of a "mature" Hemingway. After his on-and-off bouts with them, Ernest now boasted to Toby and others that he had "won after all."

With all the success, there remained the nagging problem of his divorce from Pauline. *For Whom the Bell Tolls* was openly dedicated to the new woman in his life: "This book is for Martha Gellhorn," Ernest proclaimed succinctly to the world. When Pauline divorced him on Labor Day, Ernest telegrammed a complete report of the divorce decree to Earl Adams in Key West. The telegram was to fulfill a promise he had made earlier, when Earl, who was the *Miami Herald's* bureau chief in Key West, first got wind of his marital troubles. At Ernest's request, Earl held the story until November 4, when he released it to the Associated Press wires from Miami.

Ernest and Martha were married 17 days later by a justice of the peace in Cheyenne, Wyoming, and honeymooned in New York City and Cuba. On their way back through Key West, Ernest sheepishly presented himself at his house with Sloppy Joe Russell, Joe's bartender, Skinner, and a pickup truck, and hauled most of his belongings off to the back room of Russell's bar on the corner of Duval and Greene Streets. The bundles—junk, trophy heads, guns, old clothes, and priceless manuscripts of some of his early books—remained untouched in the back room until after his death. Likely as not, Ernest never saw any of the considerable bundles again, and they would no doubt have been stolen or thrown away as junk if Toby Bruce had not made their existence known to Ernest's fourth wife, Mary Hemingway, who finally retrieved them in February of 1962.

When Ernest moved his belongings out of the house in the fall of 1940, he essentially severed all physical ties with Key West. After that time, he was literally a guest in his own home, staying in the poolhouse on his trips to and from Cuba. As one of the provisions of the divorce the Florida National Bank in Miami was appointed trustee of the Whitehead Street house. Pauline could lease or rent the house, but had to pay the taxes and insurance. If she wanted to sell the house, Ernest was to receive first choice to buy with provisions that he pay sixty percent of the asking price as a down payment. If Ernest declined to buy, he was to receive forty percent of the sale price with Pauline receiving the other sixty percent. In the event of Pauline's death the trust agreement stipulated that Patrick and Gregory would divide her sixty percent share equally, with Ernest receiving the other forty percent.

After 1940, the Key West Mob that had flourished for a full ten years would be obliged to cross the 90 miles of Gulf Stream to Ernest's new residence on the outskirts of Havana. They came at first, but it was never quite the same as it had been when they operated from Key West. Now Ernest was in every way moving off into legend. To some critics he was "the best novelist in America." Even his detractors had to admit he was the "most forceful" novelist in the country. An air, a charisma, was forming around him. For the past dozen years Ernest had been carefully carving on a gigantic wooden sign. The word was Papa. Only a handful of people would know that the lettering had been done in the island city of Key West, Florida.

He never completely lost touch with the island city: he came in and out of Key West for the next 20 years, or Toby Bruce would fly to Cuba with fishing gear, clothes, special liquors, medicines, and shotgun shells—"Papa equipment"— that the world had come to know. For 20 years after he pulled out of Key West, Ernest Hemingway lived his self-styled myth to the fullest. But by 1960 he reported to Toby Bruce that things were becoming "confused" in his head. "Nothing works right in the old machine any more," he told his old friend, referring to his body in general. Finally the myth came to be at odds with its architect, or so Hemingway believed.

On the morning of July 2, 1961, nineteen days before his sixty-second birthday, in his home in Ketchum, Idaho, Ernest Hemingway acted out the final scene of the Papa myth: he put a double-barreled shotgun to his forehead and pulled both triggers; the myth, at last, had won out.

Epilogue

After Ernest Hemingway's death on July 2, 1961, his wife Mary called a small group of family and friends together in the living room of the Ketchum house. The grisly effects of the suicide were still visible in the foyer with its walls wiped clean, its ceiling pockmarked with shot; Papa's presence was still very real: he was "on a long trip," as Toby said.

The group consisted of Mary, her lawyer, the sons—John, Patrick, and Gregory—and Toby Bruce. The discussions were personal and will have to be made public by others (though this writer was privileged to know some of them). In the end Toby was told to sell the Whitehead Street house. With the situation in Cuba deteriorating all the time, Mary resolved to clear out what she could from the Finca Vigia.

When the Key West house was put up for sale, the highest bid came from Jack H. and Bernice Dickson Daniel, former renters of the property. An "Agreement of Sale and Purchase" was signed on October 25, 1961.

Details of a 1941 trust agreement between Ernest and

Pauline became a matter of public record when Clerk Earl Adams's office recorded the agreement of sale on November 13, 1961. The trust agreement had stipulated that Ernest (or his wife) would get forty percent of the sale of the house after Pauline's death and that Patrick and Gregory would share sixty percent of the sale price.

On March 28, 1963, acting as ancillary administrator for the estate of "Ernest M. Hemingway, a deceased man," T. Otto Bruce signed for Mary Hemingway, and the 907 Whitehead Street property passed out of Hemingway hands after 32 years and eight months. The Daniels paid $32,000 for Ernest's share with a $4,800 down payment and the rest in six installments of $4,000 and a final payment of $3,200. Patrick and Gregory received $48,000 for their sixty percent share, making a total sale price of $80,000.

The Daniels lived in the main house for a short time, but curiosity seekers filtered into the grounds, seeking mementos and a glimpse at the Hemingway residence, forcing the couple to remove themselves to the poolhouse quarters and to seal off the front gate.

On January 1, 1964, under the supervision of Bernice Dickson Daniel, the main house was opened as a tourist attraction known as the Ernest Hemingway Home and Museum. For a dollar a person tourists were permitted to browse through the manicured grounds and were given a guided tour of the house and a brief, subjective run-through of Hemingway's years in the house by Mrs. Daniel's sister Frances and her husband, James Reid.

The furnishings of the house were regrouped into an approximation of the French and Spanish style pieces the Hemingways kept in the house when they lived there, with a number of the smaller pieces as actual holdover furnishings from the Hemingway days.

Mary Hemingway came back to Key West once after Papa's death. On February 12, 1962, she and Toby and Betty Bruce began filtering through and sorting Hemingway's effects left in the back room of Sloppy Joe's when he broke with Pauline for the final time and moved to Cuba in 1940. For 22 years the pile of manuscripts, books, mementos, trunks, guns, suitcases, and hunting trophies (including a bearskin rug) had gone untouched and virtually unnoticed in the back room as the property changed hands three times. Stan Smith, who owned the bar in 1962, permitted Mary Hemingway to take what she wanted from the priceless belongings, including galleys and manuscripts of *Death in the Afternoon, Green Hills of Africa,* and *To Have and Have Not.* Much of the material was turned over to the Monroe County Public Library's "Hemingway Collection," entrusted to Mrs. Bruce, the library's historian; some went to the museum of the Key West Art and Historical Association; other items were retained privately by Mrs. Hemingway.

Ernest Hemingway is now a commodity in his adopted hometown. His white, heavily bearded face is hawked on billboards and signs, his photographs displayed in restaurants and bars and on postcards. His lifestyle is still played out by many who drift into the end-of-the-line City of Key West and by countless others who read his books, see his bearded face in old magazines, or pause over it on the back flaps of Scribner's "Contemporary Classics" series. All live out the fantasies of an aging myth, the myth of a dynamically powerful and complex man—the myth of Papa.

Bibliography

Arnold, Lloyd R. *High on the Wild with Hemingway.* Caldwell,
   Idaho: The Caxton Printers, Ltd.; 1968.
Baker, Carlos. *Ernest Hemingway: A Life Story.* New York: Charles
   Scribner's Sons, 1969.
Baker, Carlos, ed. *Hemingway and his Critics.* New York: Hill &
   Wang, 1961.
Baker, Carlos. *Hemingway: The Writer as Artist.* Princeton, N.J.:
   Princeton University Press, 1952.
Benson, Jackson J. *Hemingway: The Writer's Art of Self Defense.*
   Minneapolis: University of Minnesota Press, 1969.
Bruccoli, Matthew J., ed. *Ernest Hemingway, Cub Reporter. Kansas
   City Star Stories.* Pittsburgh: University of Pittsburgh Press, 1970.
Chappick, Marie. "The Key West Story." Serialized in the Key
   West *Coral Tribune,* July 6, 1956-Aug. 22, 1958.
Dos Passos, John. *The Best Times.* New York: Signet, 1966.
Fenton, Charles A. *The Apprenticeship of Ernest Hemingway: The
   Early Years.* New York: Farrar, Straus and Cudahy, Inc., 1954.
Hemingway, Ernest. *Across the River and Into the Trees.* New York:
   Charles Scribner's Sons, 1950.

Hemingway, Ernest. *Death in the Afternoon.* New York: Charles
Scribner's Sons, 1932.

Hemingway, Ernest. *Farewell to Arms, A.* New York: Charles
Scribner's Sons, 1929.

Hemingway, Ernest. *Fifth Column and the First Forty-Nine Stories,
The.* New York: Charles Scribner's Sons, 1938.

Hemingway, Ernest. *For Whom the Bell Tolls.* New York: Charles
Scribner's Sons, 1940.

Hemingway, Ernest. *Green Hills of Africa.* New York: Charles
Scribner's Sons, 1935.

Hemingway, Ernest. *In Our Time.* New York: Boni and Liveright,
1925.

Hemingway, Ernest. *Islands in the Stream.* New York: Charles
Scribner's Sons, 1970.

Hemingway, Ernest, ed. *Men At War.* New York: Charles Scribner's
Sons, 1942.

Hemingway, Ernest. *Men Without Women.* New York: Charles
Scribner's Sons, 1927.

Hemingway, Ernest. *Moveable Feast, A.* New York: Charles Scribner's Sons, 1964.

Hemingway, Ernest. *Old Man and the Sea, The.* New York: Charles
Scribner's Sons, 1952.

Hemingway, Ernest. *Sun Also Rises, The.* New York: Charles
Scribner's Sons, 1926.

Hemingway, Ernest. *To Have and Have Not.* New York: Charles
Scribner's Sons, 1927.

Hemingway, Ernest. *Winner Take Nothing.* New York: Charles
Scribner's Sons, 1933.

Hemingway, Leicester. *My Brother Ernest Hemingway.* Cleveland:
World Publishing Co., 1962.

Hotchner, A. E. *Papa Hemingway.* New York: Random House,
1966.

Isabelle, Julianne. *Hemingway's Religious Experience,* New York:
Vantage Press, 1964.

Key West Authority. "Key West in Transition: A Guide Book
for Tourists." December 1934.

Key West *Citizen* Files, 1928-1942.

Monroe County Public Library Hemingway file. Key West, Florida.

MCaffery, John K. M., ed. *Ernest Hemingway: The Man and His Work.* Cleveland, World Publishing Co., 1950.

Montgomery, Constance Chappel. *Hemingway in Michigan.* New York: Fleet Publishing Corp., 1966.

Parks, Pat. *The Railroad That Died at Sea.* Brattleboro, Vermont: The Stephen Greene Press, 1968.

Poore, Charles, ed. *The Hemingway Reader.* New York: Charles Scribner's Sons, 1953.

Ross, Lillian. *Portrait of Hemingway.* New York: Simon and Schuster, 1961.

Samuels, Lee, comp. *A Hemingway Checklist.* New York: Charles Scribner's Sons, 1951.

Sanderson, S. F. *Ernest Hemingway.* New York: Grove Press, Inc., 1961.

Sanford, Marcelline Hemingway. *At the Hemingways: Years of Innocence.* Boston: Little, Brown and Co., 1962.

Singer, Kurt, and Sherrod, Jane. *Ernest Hemingway, Man of Courage.* Minneapolis: T. S. Denison & Co., Inc., 1963.

Stephens, Robert O. *Hemingway's Nonfiction: The Public Voice.* Chapel Hill: University of North Carolina Press, 1968.

Time Magazine. October 1, 1937. A review of *To Have and Have Not.*

White, William, ed. *By-Line: Ernest Hemingway.* New York: Charles Scribner's Sons, 1967.

Young, Philip. *Ernest Hemingway: A Reconsideration.* University Park, Pennsylvania State University Press, 1966.

Young, Philip. *Ernest Hemingway.* New York: Rinehart and Co., 1952.

Young, Philip, and Mann, Charles, eds. *The Hemingway Manuscripts: An Inventory.* University Park: Pennsylvania State University Press, 1969.

Index

Adams, Earl (Jewfish), 33, 52-53,
155, 158, 170-71, 187, 192
Adams, Hamilton (Sack of Ham),
33-35, 122, 145
Albury, Nilo, 174
Anita, the, 58, 80-81, 106, 143, 167
Allington, Floyd, 56
Arnold, Lloyd (Pappy), 180-81,
186
Arnold, Tillie, 180, 186
Baby's Place, 38, 135
Baker, Mrs. Rhoda, 35, 139
Beach, Sylvia, 98
Best Times, The (Dos Passos), 37
boxing matches, in Key West,
138-39
Brooklyn Dodgers, 121
Brooks, George (Georgie), 25-27,
32, 52, 78, 89, 102, 136, 140-43,
155
Bruce, Mrs. Betty, 192-93
Bruce, T. Otto (Toby), 46-47, 74, 78,
93, 119, 124-25, 127-28, 133-34,

136, 139-42, 149, 163, 172-79,
181-89, 191-92
Burns, Harry, 144
Cadwalader, Charles, M.B., 113-17
Carroll, Nancy, 130
Carter, Lorine Betingfield, 29
Casa Marina Hotel, 19, 37-38, 173
Castro, Fidel, 66, 101
Cates, William (Bill), 120-21, 133,
136, 140-43, 154, 162-63, 166-68,
170-71, 177
Cervantes, Octavio (Tabby), 60
de Céspedes, Carlos Manuel, 90
Chappick, Miss Marie, 82
cigar factory workers, 49
Citizen (Key West), 52, 110
Civilian Conservation Corps (CCC),
125-28, 146
Colebrooks, Alfred (Black Pie),
138-39
Coles, Jack, 144
Collier's (Magazine), 153
Colonial Hotel, 19, 31, 38, 152

Conchs, architecture, 24, 37
Cooper, Gary, 93
Cosmopolitan (magazine), 96, 131
Cuban influence on Key West, 60-65
Cuban Club, 60, 62-63, 135
Cubana Cafe, 38
Curry, Fannie, 57
"Dancing Bobby" 78-79, 86, 90
Daniel, Bernice Dickson, 191-92
Daniel, Jack H., 191
Delmonico's, 24, 40
Depression, the Great, 55-56, 62-63, 68, 77-78, 82, 104, 107-108, 134, 145-48, 156-57
Dewey, John, 16
Dos Passos, John, 20, 22, 24, 32-34, 37, 40, 42, 49, 56-57, 76, 100-02, 117, 119-20, 122-24, 144, 153, 174
Dos Passos, Kate, 76, 100, 102, 119, 122, 124
Dry Tortugas Islands, 30, 32, 39-42, 49-51, 54-56, 69, 77, 79-81, 106, 146
Dudek, Al, 100-01, 103, 117
Duncan, B. M., 109-10, 113
El Pacifico, 116
Esquire (magazine), 88-89, 98, 130
Evansville Courier (Indiana), 130
Federal Emergency Relief Administration (FERA), 110-13
Finca Vigia (La Vigia), 101, 178, 182-83, 191
Finnegans Wake (Joyce), 91
Fitzgerald, F. Scott, 32, 48-49
Flagler, Henry, 21, 37
Florida East Coast Railroad, 21, 23, 31, 33, 38, 42-43, 51, 62, 100, 108, 126-28
Forbes, Kermit (Battl'n Geech), 138-39
Fort Jefferson, 40-42, 50, 54, 59, 80, 146
Fort Taylor, 19, 114

Fourie, Ben, 94
Fowler, Dr. Henry, 113, 115-17
Franklin, Sidney, 117-18, 153, 156, 161
Franco, Gen. Francisco, 153, 173
Fuentes, Gregorio, 59
Gabrielle (nurse), 76, 78
gambling, Key West, 53, 60-66
Gellhorn, Martha, see Hemingway, Martha
Gibson Hotel, 38
Gilfond, M. E., 113
Gingrich, Arnold, 88, 130, 132
Gomez, Judge Arthur (Kitty), 184-5
Gutiérrez, Capt. Carlos, 50-51, 81, 106-7, 114-17, 132
Habana Madrid, 61, 168
Hamilton, Bill, 180
Hemingway, Carol, 58,83
Hemingway, Dr. Clarence, 22-24, 48
Hemingway, Ernest
Chronology: Arrives in Key West, 19. John Dos Passos recommends Key West, 20. Rents first residence in Key West, 21-22. Fishing, the lure of, 25. Meets Charles Thompson, 25. Forms Key West Mob, 33-34. Leaves Key West first time, 43. Birth of Patrick, 46. Meets Toby Bruce, 46-47. Rents second residence in Key West, 48. Leaves Key West second time, 53. Rents third residence in Key West, 53. Seeks permanent residence in Key West, 55. Leaves Key West third time, 55. Rents fourth residence in Key West, 57. Decides to settle in Key West, 67-68. Birth of Gregory, 71. Buys house, 69, 73-76. Postpones African safari, 79. Domestic staff is assembled, 78-79. Begins *Esquire* "Letters," 88. African

Hemingway, Ernest (cont.)
safari, 90-96. Buys *Pilar,* 98. Pilar described, 99-02. Takes *Pilar* on first extended cruise, 113-18. Takes *Pilar* to Bimini, 122-24 Toby Bruce builds brick wall, 124-25. Inspects 1935 Labor Day hurricane disaster area, 127. Begins "Harry Morgan" stories, 88, 96, 130, 140. *To Have and Have Not* characters partially detailed, 143-48. Daily routine in Key West, 134-38, Meets Martha Gellhorn, 149-51. Involvement in Spanish Civil War: first trip, 153-54; second trip, 160-61; third trip, 163-64; fourth trip, 172-73. Installed as "Papa", 154-55. Love triangle with Pauline H. and Martha Gellhorn (as revealed in *To Have and Have Not*), 158-60; (as revealed in *The Fifth Column*), 160-61. Breaks with Pauline, moves to Cuba with Martha Gellhorn, 177. Goes to Sun Valley, Idaho, 179. Forms Sun Valley Mob, 180. Final break with Pauline, 181-82. Begins permanent move to Cuba, 182. Pauline obtains divorce, 184-85. Marries Martha Gellhorn, 188. Collects belongings in Key West and moves to Cuba, 188. Death in Idaho, 189.
Books: Death in the Afternoon, 56, 71, 73-74, 76, 81-84, 86-87, 129, 157, 193
Farewell to Arms, A, 22-23, 30, 34, 39, 46-49, 51, 53, 87, 130, 157
Fifth Column and the First Forty-nine Stories, The, 171-72
For Whom the Bell Tolls, 17, 74, 121, 174-75, 177, 180, 182-83, 186-87

Green Hills of Africa, 27, 74, 100, 102-03, 114, 118-20, 122, 125, 129-31, 151, 154, 157, 193
Islands in the Stream, 122-23
Men without Women, 28, 36, 46, 157
Moveable Feast, A, 91
Old Man and the Sea, The, 17, 42, 59, 115, 173
Sun Also Rises, The, 28, 36, 157
To Have and Have Not, 27, 37, 67, 74, 88, 96, 102, 121, 127, 132-33, 137, 140, 143-48, 150, 154-57, 160, 193
Winner Take Nothing, 74, 77, 89, 96, 157
Film: Spanish Earth, The, 74
Play: Fifth Column, The, 74, 122, 160-62
Short Stories: "After the Storm," 41, 77, "Short Happy Life of Francis Macomber, The," 74, 131, 176 "Snows of Kilimanjaro, The," 74, 132
Hemingway, Grace Hall, 22-24, 58, 83, 173
Hemingway, Gregory Hancock, 71, 76, 79, 82-83, 85, 87, 90, 97, 124, 132-35, 140, 161, 166, 174, 178, 184-85, 188, 191-92
Hemingway, Hadley, 24, 46, 179
Hemingway, John (Bumby), 46, 48, 53, 55-56, 87, 174, 185, 191
Hemingway, Leicester (Les), 83, 100-03, 106, 117
Hemingway, Madelaine (Sunny), 48-49
Hemingway, Martha, 17, 148, 149-54, 156, 158-61, 163-64, 165-66, 171-73, 177-188
Hemingway, Mary, 188, 191-93
Hemingway, Patrick, 46-48, 53, 55-56, 71, 76, 78-79, 82-83, 87, 90, 97, 124-25, 132-34, 140, 161, 166,

Hemingway, Patrick (cont.)
    174, 178, 184-85, 188, 191-92
Hemingway, Pauline, 17, 20-25, 29-
    33, 42, 45-49, 53-57, 68-72, 73-
    79, 81-87, 89-98, 100-02, 113,
    115, 119, 124, 128, 132-35, 139-
    40, 149-56, 158-61, 163-64, 165-
    66, 168-70, 172-74, 177-79, 181-
    88, 192-93
Hemingway, Ursula, 90, 131-32
Hemingway House, Key West,
    191-92
Herrmann, John, 54, 58-59
Hepburn, Ina, 78, 82, 90
Herlihy, James, 16
Higgs, Carrie Woods, 29
Holiday (Hemingway quote), 99-100
"Hoover Gold," 36, 64; see also
    Prohibition
Horne, Bill, 47
Hurricane, Labor Day 1935, 125-28,
    140, 144
International News (Baltimore), 52
Isabelle, 78-79, 83, 86, 89-90, 134
Jennings, Jenny, 175-76
Jennings, John, 175
Joyce, James, 91, 98
Kelly ("Shipwreck"), 176-77
Ken (Magazine), 163
Kerchiner, Otto, 82
Ketchum, Idaho, 189-91
Key, Jakie, 33
Key West Authority (KWA), 110-
    113, 118, 124-25, 144-45
"Key West Rhythm," 67
"Key West Story, The" (Chappick),
    82
"Key West in Transition, A Guide
    Book for Tourists," 112-13
L-Bar-T Ranch, Wyoming, 27, 56-
    57, 85-87, 132, 178-80
Laughton, James, 144
Laurie, Victor, 138-39
Lanham, Col. (later Gen.) Charles

Truman (Buck), 93
Lester, J. Lancelot, 109
Lowe, Joe, 144
Lowry, Malcolm, 46
Lowry, Ruth, 46
Lund, Charles, 113-14
Machado, Gerardo, 90
McGrath, Father, 103-04
MacLeish, Ada, 100
MacLeish, Archibald, 32, 102-03,
    174
Malone, Mayor William H., 69, 109-
    110
Mason, Jane, 130
Miami Herald, 52, 104, 187
Matthews, Herbert, 172
McGuane, Thomas, 16
Mills, Joe, 138
Monroe County Public Library, 193
Morales, Arthur, 38
Morning Journal (Key West), 52
Mulberg Chevrolet Co. of Key West,
    133
Murphy, Gerald, 100-02
Murphy, Sara, 100-02
New Deal, 67, 109, 112, 128, 144-47
New Masses, The (magazine), 127
Nordquist, Lawrence, 57, 84
Nordquist, Olive, 57, 84
North American Newspaper Alliance
    (NANA), 153, 160, 163
Olive (baby sitter), 48
Ordonez, Antonio, 93
Overseas Highway, 43, 111, 128
Overseas Hotel, 34, 38
"Papa Dobles" (rum drink), 150
Peirce, Waldo, 33-34, 39, 41, 49,
    130, 174
Pena's Garden of Roses, 38, 63, 70,
    135, 151
Percival, Phillip, 93-96, 102, 129
Perkins, Maxwell, 49, 51, 53-54, 59,
    76, 84, 86-87, 96, 125, 160, 172,
    174, 183-84

Pfeiffer, Gustavus, 21, 45, 68-70, 77, 89
Pfeiffer, Mary, 45
Pfeiffer, Paul, 31-32, 43, 45
Pfeiffer, Virginia (Jinny), 75-76, 78, 90, 184
Phoebe (cook), 28, 35, 78
Pilar, the, 51, 81, 98, 99-107, 113-118, 120, 122, 124-25, 127, 130, 132, 139-40, 142, 155, 161, 163, 170-71, 178, 183
Pinder, Albert (Bread), 59-60, 122, 145
Pinder, Sam B., 109
Prohibition, 38, 61, 87, 106
Prostitution in Key West, 63, 66-67
Ramon's, 38
Raul's, 38, 63, 135
Reynolds, Quentin, 170-71
Roberts, James (Iron Baby), 137-38
Ross, Lillian, 17
Russell, Anita, 120-21
Russell, Joe, 33, 36-37, 58, 76, 80-82, 87-88, 101, 106-107, 115, 119-21, 130-31, 133, 136, 140, 143-45, 149-50, 154, 163, 167-68, 174, 188
Russell, Joe Jr., 167-68
Rutherford, Hugo, 176
safari, African, 28, 55-56, 74, 77, 84, 89-96, 131
St. Bede's Catholic Church, Key West, 158
Samuelson, Arnold (Mice), 104-106, 112, 115-16, 118
Samber, Larry, 137-38
Saunders, Burge, 33, 39, 49-51, 54, 58-59
Saunders, Eddie (Capt. Bra), 30, 33, 39-42, 49-51, 58, 76-77, 79-80, 93, 100-01, 127, 144
Scribner's (magazine), 49, 122
Shepard, Mrs. Arthur, 82
Scribner, Charles, Sr., 93

Scribner's (publishers), 36, 47-51, 53, 77, 86, 88, 122, 156, 163, 166, 184, 187, 193
Shevlin, Tommy, 176
Shipman, Evan, 153
Sholtz, Dave, 107, 109
Skinner (bartender), 120, 136, 149-50, 188
Sloppy Joe's Bar: first location, 33, 36, 60, 70; second location, 106, 119-22, 133, 135-36, 140-42, 146, 149-51, 162; third location, 162, 167, 170-71, 176-77, 193
Smith, Bill, 33-34, 40-41, 174
Smith, Jimmy, 78, 83, 86, 90, 181-82
Smith, Stan, 193
Spackman, Spike, 180
Spottswood, Mary Lou, 169
Stengel, Casey, 121
Stern, Ada, 79, 82-83, 87, 90, 124, 132, 134, 161, 169-70
Stevens, Wallace, 52, 130-31
Stone, Julius F., Jr., 109-13
Strater, Henry (Mike), 33, 39, 48-49, 54, 122-23
Sullivan, J. B. (Sully), 33, 58, 76, 89, 101, 127, 129, 136, 155, 163, 174
Sun Valley, Idaho, 93, 179-81, 184-86
Taylor, Henry, 184
Thompson, Charles, 24-30, 32-35, 39-40, 42-43, 47-49, 51, 53-59, 68, 70, 76, 79-81, 83-86, 89-97, 100-02, 104-05, 117, 119-20, 122-23, 129, 136, 150-52, 154-55, 163, 165, 168-70, 174, 184
Thompson, Karl, 24, 27
Thompson, Lorine, 25, 27-31, 33, 42-43, 48, 51, 53, 55-60, 68-71, 74-76, 78-79, 81, 83-84, 90, 92-93, 96-98, 117, 119, 124, 150-52, 156, 161, 165-66, 168-70, 174, 183-85
Thompson, Norberg, 24
Tift, Asa, 70

Time (magazine), 156-57
Treadway, C. E., 113
Trevor, Jerry, 69
Trevor and Morris Apartments, 21-23, 31
Trevor and Morris Company, 21
Tropical Club, 38, 135
Trumbo Club, 135
Trouble I've Seen, The (Gellhorn), 149
Val Banera, the, 41, 77
Valladares, Arthur, 36
Valladares, Leonte, 36
Valladares Book Store, 35-36
Vanderbilt, Alfred, 96
Van Guilder, Gene, 180

Vasquez, Raul, 38
La Vigia (renamed Finca Vigia), 101, 178, 182-83, 191
Von Blixen, Baron, 95-96
Warren, Leo H., 109
Warren, Mrs. William R., 111
Weaver, Chub, 58-59, 85
What Happens (Herrmann), 54
What Mad Pursuit (Gellhorn), 149
Whitmarsh, Mary F., 69
Williams, Joe, 121
Williams, Miriam, 134-35, 138, 152
Williams, Taylor, 93, 180-81, 186
Williams, Tennessee, 16
Wolkowsky, Isaac, 162
World Telegram (New York), 121

JUN 0 7 2024